Anchored in Freedom

Gina Fox

ANCHORED IN FREEDOM: Turning Trials Into Testimonies of Triumph

Copyright © 2024 GINA FOX

All rights reserved. No part of this publication may be reproduced or transmitted in any form without the prior written permission of the publisher and contributors, except in the case of brief quotations or critical reviews.

Scripture quotations marked NKJV are taken from the New King James Version®. Copyright ©1982 by Thomas Nelson. Used by permission. All rights reserved.
Scripture quotations marked (NIV) are taken from the Holy Bible, New International Version®, NIV®. Copyright © 1973, 1978, 1984, 2011 by Biblica, Inc.™ Used by permission of Zondervan. All rights reserved worldwide. www.zondervan.com The "NIV" and "New International Version" are trademarks registered in the United States Patent and Trademark Office by Biblica, Inc.™
Scripture quotations marked NLT are taken from the Holy Bible, New Living Translation, copyright ©1996, 2004, 2007, 2013 by Tyndale House Foundation. Used by permission of Tyndale House Publishers, Inc., Carol Stream, Illinois 60188. All rights reserved.
Scripture quotations marked MSG are taken from THE MESSAGE, copyright © 1993, 2002, 2018 by Eugene H. Peterson. Used by permission of Nav Press, represented by Tyndale House Publishers. All rights reserved.
Scripture quotations marked ESV are from the Holy Bible, English Standard Version, copyright © 2001, 2007, 2011, 2016 by Crossway Bibles, a division of Good News Publishers. Used by permission. All rights reserved.
Scripture quotations marked CSB have been taken from the Christian Standard Bible®, Copyright © 2017 by Holman Bible Publishers. Used by permission. Christian Standard Bible® and CSB® are federally registered trademarks of Holman BiblePublishers.

Edited by: Sarah Geringer
Formatted by: Ruth Hovsepian
Interior and Cover Designs: Michelle Gautreaux
Cover and internal art done using Canva Pro
Author Photo: Khloe Velton

ANCHORED IN FREEDOM

GINA FOX

CONTENTS

Praise for Anchored in Freedom	vii
Dedication	x
Foreword	xiii
Book Music Playlist	xv
Podcast Episode Playlist	xvi
Introduction	xvii

SECTION 1: Mental Health — 1

  1. The Lines Are Drawn *by Gina Fox* — 3
  2. The Glory of Love *by Jodi Howe* — 11
  3. The Fight of My Life *by Scott Box* — 19
  4. The Mind of Christ *by Kim Gentry Meyer* — 27
  5. Symbols of Hope *by Cally Logan* — 37
  6. Living and Active Help *by Wendy Blight* — 45

SECTION 2: Grief and Loss — 53

  7. Empty Arms, Full Heart *by Gina Fox* — 55
  8. I Surrender All *by Grace Klein* — 63
  9. Overcoming the Deep Waters *by Amy Joob* — 73
  10. Taking Authority Over Grief *by Lacy Grace* — 81

SECTION 3: Survival — 91

  11. Surviving the Hills and Valleys *by Gina Fox* — 93
  12. Surviving Hell to Find Hope *by Brit Eaton* — 103
  13. Surviving the Darkest Valleys *by Christa Crookston* — 111
  14. Surviving the Critics *by Kat Vazquez* — 119
  15. Surviving Addiction *by George A. Wood* — 127

16. Surviving the False Narratives *by Lindsay Griswold*   141

17. Healing From Body Shame *by Heather Creekmore*   151

SECTION 4: Healing   161

18. Jesus is the Answer *by Micah Lynn Hanson*   163

19. Healing From Fear *by Elle Cardel*   175

20. Falling Into Surrender *by Benny DiChiara*   183

21. Healing From Shame *by Inés Franklin*   191

22. Healing Is Not Just Physical *by Gina Fox*   201

Conclusion   213

Acknowledgments   217

Special Thanks   220

Contributor Information   221

About Gina Fox and Anchored by the Sword   227

Praise for Anchored in Freedom

"So often depression, anxiety, and other mental illnesses feel like a dirty rag we must hide away and never reveal to another living soul. We often suffer in silence, but Gina seeks to shed some light, some holy light upon these topics. Through her own courageous story and the real, tangible, and raw stories of others, *Anchored in Freedom* opens the door to a safe place. Vulnerability fosters connection, and Gina does just that. This book is a conduit of heaven to remind you that you are not alone in this; you have a gracious and loving Heavenly Lord Who can sympathize with you, and you are not the only one who has struggled before. Find freedom, catharsis, and camaraderie in this powerful book."

—**CALLY LOGAN**, Author of *Hang in There, Girl, Dear Future Husband* and *The Wallflower That Bloomed*

"What happens when our stories don't unfold the way we thought they would? When our dreams become unraveled, and our hope is tossed about by waves of uncertainty? Anchored to the wrong thing — or the wrong *one* — our faith is rocked, and our hope is swept away. Maybe you're in this place of chaos now.

What we need is an Anchor who secures us and holds us above the waves of defeat. **Anchored in Freedom** is a compilation of real stories from real people who wrestle with real struggles – and have tethered their trust to an unsinkable Anchor — Jesus.

Gina Fox invites you to ride the swells of each freedom story, looking for hidden gems that will inspire hope as you reflect on thought-provoking questions. Gina's vulnerability and easy style make this book a win-win for anyone who needs to strengthen their hope."

—**STEFANIE LIBERTORE**, Author of *Unbound: Heal, Reclaim, Unleash*

"Gina is doing the near impossible: she's building an authentic community around one of the hardest topics in Christendom: mental health. You need only to open the pages of this book to see and feel the impact of her talent and courage.

If you've ever felt alone in the battle for a healthy mind (and who hasn't?!), these faith-filled stories are for you.

The world needs this book, and the world needs Gina. I'm very grateful for both."

—**KIM GENTRY MEYER**, Singer-Songwriter, Album — *Herald*

"*Anchored in Freedom* is an authentic, relatable, and inspirational collection of stories from men and women who turned their past seasons of suffering into permanent souvenirs of success. Gina's encouragement, along with the biblical principles and verses within these pages, will be both a blessing and a balm to the hearts of readers feeling heartbroken or hopeless. This book will enable those feeling trapped by their trials to view their circumstances through the lens of God's goodness, proving that they too can turn their own seasons of suffering into testimonies of triumph, remaining anchored in the presence of God no matter how rough the stormy seasons of life they face this side of heaven becomes."

—**TRACY STEEL**, Women's Ministry Director, Speaker, and Author of *A Redesigned Life: Uncovering God's Purpose When Life Doesn't Go As Planned* (Revell, 2019)

"Gina and her fellow authors are familiar with pain and suffering, yet they also know the importance of clinging to faith in hard times. These stories are real, gritty, and heartfelt, which will validate and affirm you in the trenches of your struggles. This book offers practical help for your hurts as well as biblically sound reasons to cling to hope through stories of these warriors of faith."

—**SARAH GERINGER**, editor, creative coach, book launch manager, artist, and author of seven books, including ***Hope for the Hard Days: 100 Encouraging Devotions***

Dedication

I dedicate this book to three women who had a major influence on my life and why I am who I am today.

My mother, **Theresa Payne**. We had a lot of difficulties and trials due to mental health issues in both of us, especially as I was becoming an adult. You taught me some very valuable lessons that I carry with me today, including the power of persistence, fighting for what you believe in and not being afraid to step out of your comfort zone. I watched you do all of these things in different areas of your life until you gave into the life that bipolar disorder forced you to live. I'm still sorry that you couldn't fight off those demons, no matter how hard you tried.

My grandmother, **Virginia Payne**. You were the greatest example of being a wife and a Christian that I had growing up and into my early adulthood. You carried a quiet confidence and when you spoke, people straightened up to hear what you had to say. You kept your Bible and devotional books on the table and did nothing else until you spent time with God. You did this every day until the cancer took its toll and you could no longer stay awake enough. I miss hearing your voice, asking you questions, and having our talks as we were watching game shows or shopping. Thank you for being the one I could lean on when I had no one else. I love you!

My mentor and friend, **Margaret Reaves**. Although we didn't know each other long or very well, you were always someone I could come to when I had questions about my faith or needed prayer. I will never forget our conversation in December of 2019. I would not be here if it wasn't for that conversation and this book would not be in the hands of the person reading it. When I reached a crossroads with a few situations and asked you to pray for me, you said, "I will pray for you and with you, but you already know what to do, and you just need to do it." I have carried these words through starting Anchored by the Sword, the podcast and in many other facets of my life. I am not perfect at it by a long shot, but those words hang on the door to my library office to remind me of why I do what I do. You were one of my biggest supporters, and I am still sad that your story is not on my episode list. I am so grateful for the time we spent together.

Foreword

In this world, we will all experience pain. Jesus warned us we would (John 16:33). But he also offered the assurance that we could take heart because he has overcome the world. Our pain and suffering take many forms. For some, it's physical. For others, it's emotional, mental, or relational. Still others may experience spiritual pain, which leaves them feeling disconnected from God or his mercy, love, compassion, or forgiveness. To make matters worse, many of us will also simultaneously experience secondary pain, which is the pain inflicted by the words or actions of others (or lack thereof), which only serves to make the pain sufferer feel worse in their already painful condition. God never intended for us to suffer, and I believe he hurts when his children hurt. He promises that he is close to us when we are brokenhearted (Psalm 34:18), and he longs to comfort us in our suffering and heal our painful condition.

If we aren't experiencing physical, emotional, relational, or spiritual pain now, either we recently have, we likely soon will, or we are walking alongside someone in the trenches who wonders if they will survive. It isn't a matter of if we will hurt, but when and how, and more importantly, what will we do with our pain. Will we run away from God in our anger, discouragement, and defiance, or will we run to him for his safe shelter and comfort? Because we serve a good and redemptive God, he never wastes our pain or our past. Romans 8:28 is often used as a "Bible verse Band-Aid" of sorts, a panacea to make the pain sufferer feel better somehow about their suffering. Yet, it contains such an important truth that we often miss it when it's thrown at us a bit flippantly: God is so good that he brings good from our suffering. He offers beauty for our ashes and sacred scars for our painful wounds. What the enemy intended to harm us, God will use for good! (Genesis 50:20)

Whether our pain is physical, emotional, relational, or spiritual, we long to know someone understands, that someone cares, and that we aren't alone in our struggle. We need the stories of others to encourage our hearts to remind us to hold on when everything in us wants to run, hide, or give up. In the pages of this book, real people share about real painful trials and real testimonies of how God saw them through. Their stories reflect their sacred scars that represent the tapestry of God's healing in their lives to encourage you in yours. Their stories epitomize the scripture that encourages us to comfort others with the same comfort God has shown to us (2 Corinthians 1:4). In doing so, it reflects a redemptive purpose for our pain.

Scripture reminds us that where the spirit of the Lord is, there is freedom (2 Corinthians 3:17). Freedom is found in a relationship with a God who loves us too much to leave us where we are and promises his very presence with us every step of the way. As you pursue the Lord and his healing and comfort for your painful trials, you will be set free and have a story of freedom to share with someone else who needs it!

Hope Prevails,
Dr. Michelle Bengtson
Board Certified Clinical Neuropsychologist,
Host of Your Hope Filled Perspective Podcast
author of many award-winning books, including *The Hem of His Garment: Reaching Out to God When Pain Overwhelms* and *Sacred Scars: Resting in God's Promise That Your Past is Not Wasted*

Book Music Playlist

I am personally obsessed with music. I can listen to a song and I can remember an exact emotion or experience involving that song. If you are on my email list, you know I include songs to listen to with each email. I wanted to include some songs that inspired me when I was putting this book together.

Scan the QR code below to find the list.

Podcast Episode Playlist

Instead of including separate QR codes for each chapter, I have created a playlist that contains each episode to correlate with each chapter. After you are done reading their story, you can come back here and listen to the rest of their stories.

Scan the QR code below to find the list.

Introduction

How many times have you wondered why you are still here? How did you survive that situation? The abuse, the addiction, or the thing that was meant to take you out, yet you are still here. Friends, there is a reason you are and His name is God. God has a plan for your life, whether you believe it or not. You could have this book in your hands because someone gave it to you, or you found it at your local store and thought the cover was cute. Or maybe someone you know has contributed to it. Whatever the reason is, it was not an accident. If no one has told you, ***you are loved!*** You were made on purpose, for a purpose, at this very time in history. Your life has meaning. There is nothing you have done that can keep you from God. He already knows it and He still sent His Son to die on a cross for your sins and for mine.

I do not claim to know everything, and neither do the people who contributed to this book, but what each one of us can say is we were lost and now we are found. We were once blind and now we can see. We have each experienced freedom in our own lives and now we want to share it with you. Each of the contributors will share a snippet of their story and there is a playlist at the beginning of the book for you to scan and listen to the rest of their stories. Then I have written a devotional based on one of their anchor verses the contributor chose for the podcast episode.

I am so glad this book found its way into your hands! Please know you have a book full of people who may not know you personally but are praying for your eyes to be opened and that you will come to experience the true freedom each of us has found through the saving grace of our God.

SECTION 1

Mental Health

Mental health is something many of us have dealt with in one way, shape or form. We've seen it in our family, our friendships, or even in ourselves. For some of us, it includes all of these and more. There are so many different struggles that people have which can include everything from anxiety and depression to suicide attempts. In this section, each individual will share their account of how mental illness has impacted their life and how God can use even something that the world and the church still want to throw a label on and say doesn't truly exist. I invite you to read and then listen to each person's testimony. Even if it isn't your story, you will gain more empathy for others who struggle with these issues.

Chapter 1

The Lines Are Drawn

by Gina Fox

Mental illness has plagued my family for generations, primarily the women on my mom's side of the family. Each woman struggled with varying degrees of bipolar disorder, but nobody talked about it or did anything about it. It stirred anger that would divide mother from daughter and grandmother from granddaughter for years at a time. This came to a head for my mom and I.

Growing up, we stayed away from my grandmother when she and my mom would fight. I hated being away from grandma because I loved both of them and didn't want to take sides. I knew there was something wrong with my mom, but I didn't understand what was going on. As I grew up, we grew further apart. She told me that she didn't want our relationship to be like the one she had with her mother, but that is exactly what we had.

Mental illness ripped my family apart by stealing the best parts of my mom away from us. She sought out care from a physician who seemed more concerned about getting paid and handing out drugs rather than figuring out how to truly help her. I was forced to live a lot of time away from her because the toxicity was affecting my own physical, mental, relational and spiritual health.

My personal journey with mental illness started at a young age. I was depressed after dealing with years of physical sickness, bullying at school and issues in my family. At the age of 12, I was so depressed that I attempted suicide by using a slap bracelet. Now this did nothing to me, but I was so down that I didn't care. I just needed to feel something real. I didn't tell anyone about that for a long time. The last time I contemplated suicide was 23 years later in 2014. I will go into more of what happened in chapter 11, but the Holy Spirit rescued me on that day and I have spent the last decade discovering why.

In 2020, while the whole world was on lockdown, I spent my quarantine addressing and working through my life's trauma—not only things that happened to me, but things that I had done to others. With everything that came to the surface, I realized that I had to focus on my mental health if I ever wanted to overcome the issues and struggles that had plagued me for over 25 years. During that process, my healing began. It continues to this day, because as my friend, Stefanie says, "We are healed and we are healing." It is a daily process with many facets, all revealed in their own timing.

So began my journey with God for my healing. Some parts of this journey may make people uncomfortable, but so will others who write their stories, so I will go first.

I have been taking anti-depressant medications for years now. I was also taking medication for anxiety until September 2021, when with the assistance of my doctor, I weaned off the medication. I have been in counseling since March 2022 with an amazing Christian counselor who has helped me continue on a journey that has led me to a place where I can write out parts of my story.

I take meds, see a counselor and love Jesus. I believe that someone can do all of this. I have been through hills and valleys with every part of my life, but I am in the best place I have ever been in. I believe that God can miraculously heal; I have seen it in my own life. But I also believe that He can lead us on a journey to wholeness and wellness. The key phrase there is "lead us." Even when I walked away from Him, He never left me. His hand has been on my life through it all. He does the same with you, even if you don't know Him.

Does God cause mental illness or make people sick? No. We live in a fallen imperfect world He never wanted for us. But can He use terrible, awful things for good? Yes. We will not have full understanding of these things on this side of heaven, but we can trust Him with all of it.

Mental illness can be our own personal hell on earth, consuming us from the inside out. It can cause us to sink into the furthest hole and feel like we have been discarded and left for dead. It can feel like the unseen version of leprosy within the church. It is not always something that can be prayed away or cast out. There can be physiological things taking place in our brains that are not working right. Things like undealt trauma, abuse, addiction and other things can contribute to it as well. We need to look at the person as a whole and not shove them in a category or make them feel bad about themselves. They get enough of that. The way to help someone who lives with mental health issues is to love them, lead them to people and resources to help them, and most of all, lead them to Jesus. This isn't a self-help book, but I know what has helped me. I wish my mom would have discovered it before it was too late.

Reflection with Gina:

> "You intended to harm me, but God intended it for good to accomplish what is now being done, the saving of many lives."
>
> —Genesis 50:20 (NLT)

Mental health is something with which many of us struggle, whether it's personally or through someone close to us. Living with mental health challenges can often feel like a battle for which we weren't prepared for. The thoughts, emotions, and behaviors that come with these challenges can be overwhelming and isolating. It's easy to feel as though the world, and sometimes even our own minds, are working against us.

But as Genesis 50:20 reminds us even in the darkest of times, God is working behind the scenes, turning what was meant for harm into something good. It's not always easy to see this in the moment, especially when we're in the thick of it. However, God's promise is that He is with us, using even our struggles to accomplish something greater.

When it comes to mental health, it's crucial to seek the help and support we need. This might mean therapy, medication, or simply having someone to talk to who understands. It's also important to recognize that God's hand is at work, even when things seem bleak. He can use our struggles to strengthen us, help us grow, and equip us to help others who are going through similar challenges.

In drawing boundaries and seeking the right help, we are not only protecting ourselves but also opening the door for God to work in our lives.

We must remember that our worth is not diminished by our struggles and that God can turn even the most difficult circumstances into something that brings life and hope to others.

Questions:

1. How has your experience with mental health challenges shaped your understanding of God's presence and purpose in your life?

2. In what ways can you seek God's strength and guidance while also taking practical steps to care for your mental health?

3. How can you use your journey with mental health to support and encourage others who might be going through similar struggles?

Prayer:

God, thank you for being with me on this life journey. It hasn't been easy, but I know and trust You in all things. Reveal to me the ways You have led me through the hardest times in my life and how they have been used to help others. You know how I am still struggling; help me to seek You and other resources and people You have placed in my life so that I can become more whole with and in You. Show me people I can help, too. In Jesus's name, Amen.

"You intended to harm me, but God intended it for good to accomplish what is now being done, the saving of many lives."

GENESIS 50:20
(NLT)

Chapter 2

The Glory of Love

By Jodi Howe

I have been writing out my testimony for over 12 years. It amazes me just how much it can change, and God shows little snippets of how He has been faithful and how He has kept His promises. The main story remains: "I once was blind, and now I can see!"

I've dealt with anxiety for the majority of my life, but it hit me like a ton of bricks around the time I was getting ready to turn 40 years old. It came out of nowhere and didn't make any sense. My days consisted of general anxiety over nothing. I felt like the world was closing in on me, and I was unable to find peace no matter what I tried. Fear overpowered my mind and my spirit. It got worse each day to the point where it eventually took over my ability to even function. I never knew anxiety could be that powerful! It wasn't until I got so mentally and physically ill that I had to seek help both physically and spiritually.

My mother began to fear for my life and decided to come over to my home to attempt to help in the only way she knew how: love and action. She asked me if I would see a friend she had known. I also knew this friend, but just in passing. Our friend wasn't a mental health provider and knew very little about mental illness, but she knew Jesus. The Holy Spirit told my mother that I needed to go and be in her presence.

As I walked into her home, I felt awkward because we had never sat down and had a conversation. Before we spoke, she was on the phone with her sister, a firm believer, who was dying from many ailments, yet they were praying for me. I didn't know or understand anything about prayer and the power it holds. We spoke about life for a while, and then it was time for me to leave. She was insistent on praying for me and asked me if I would want to start a Bible study with her. I thought that was odd and uncomfortable, but I felt led to say yes. I can look back now and see that tug, that pursuance, was Jesus Christ. Jesus showed up and embraced me in ways that I couldn't have ever imagined.

It took many months to feel at peace with my anxiety. I worked through it using God and His Word, as well as utilizing other methods God provided through Western medicine, therapy, and acceptance. Walking through anxiety can be very scary and can make you feel nervous and unsettled, especially if you have ever experienced a panic attack. A panic attack can feel as though you're having a heart attack and can be so strong that it takes your breath away.

But they are not as strong and powerful as our Lord and Savior, Jesus Christ!

As I started to build a foundation of knowledge and wisdom of anxiety, I learned of ways to deal with it as a thorn in my flesh with sufficient grace. Although you can still have bouts of anxiety, you can certainly heal from it and live the abundant life that God promises us.

The valleys and the mountains have been consistent during my walk with Christ, but I can tell you that the Word of God has been my lifeline and my anchor.

One scripture that has been vital to me is Proverbs 3:5–6: *"Trust in the Lord, with all your heart and lean not on your own understanding. Acknowledge him in all your ways, and he will set your paths straight."*

I first learned that scripture in my early walks with Jesus, and it has stuck with me for over a decade of highs and lows and everything in between. What is most beautiful about this verse and, frankly, all of God's Word, is that you can look back and see how it applies to everyday life. Even when you are walking through the valley of the shadow of death, that trust in Him sustains you. He is our Rod & Staff! He is the Prince of Peace. He is the only way, truth, and life. Confidence in our flesh is unsustainable. But trust in him is a game changer in feeling peace that surpasses understanding.

These last few years have been the hardest in my life. They've consisted of loss, divorce, financial hardship, a daughter who can't accept her identity as a beautiful female child of God, and so on. I've cried in the corner of my closet and tried to smile during the struggles. Although it hasn't been easy, His grace has been sufficient through all of it. We are not guaranteed an easy life. Jesus tells us that this world will give us trouble but that he has overcome the world (John 16:33). So our struggles are entirely under the wings of His protection and power. Trusting in Him with our hearts is a muscle that takes time to develop. As you grow, it will become easier to remove the urge to lean on anything but God. Having a clear vision that everything the world has tried to tell us directly opposes His perfect plan for our lives.

I have discovered joy amid all the pain and struggles I have experienced. Through constant gratitude, I can tell you God continues to set my broken roads straight and always leads me back to Him. I'm learning in life that peace is not the absence of problems but the presence of God. I know now more than ever that while I'm here, I do not want to live without him. I will do everything in my minuscule powers to hang tight to His love and promises because He is the author of my story, and He has the ability to make it a masterpiece. That's my story, and that's the glory of love from God.

Reflection with Gina:

> "Don't worry about anything, but in everything, through prayer and petition with thanksgiving, present your requests to God. And the peace of God, which surpasses all understanding, will guard your hearts and minds in Christ Jesus."
>
> —Philippians 4:6–7 (CSB)

In this verse, Paul is reminding the church of Philippi to look first to God for everything they need. He is encouraging them to walk out their faith journey without wondering where everything they need to live is sourced. There is no need for them to feel anxious when they come to Him in prayer and with gratitude. The God who created each of us knows exactly what we need to get through the day. When we try to handle things on our own and look to the left and the right, our minds become confused and anxious. The world we live in today is full of confusing messages that encourage us to do everything for ourselves. While we need to work and walk in the calling He has for us, it is our job to keep our eyes on Him. He's got us!

Questions:

1. When was the last time you felt overwhelmed by worry or anxiety? How did turning to prayer and thanksgiving shift your perspective?

2. What are some specific ways you can keep your eyes on God and trust in His provision, even when the world around you is confusing?

Prayer:

God, I come to you today with so much anxiety and stress filling my head and heart. I admit I don't always come to You first, if ever. Please forgive me. Right now, I open my hands, my heart, and my mind to you and ask You to take control. As I am handing over all of my needs to You, I am truly grateful that You know exactly what I need to get through the next minute, hour, day, etc. When I forget, bring me back to You. I am so thankful for the blessed assurance I have in You as my provider and my comforter. I thank you for the perfect peace only You can provide. In Jesus's name, Amen.

"Don't worry about anything, but in everything, through prayer and petition with thanksgiving, present your requests to God. And the peace of God, which surpasses all understanding, will guard your hearts and minds in Christ Jesus."

PHILIPPIANS 4:6-7
(CSB)

Chapter 3

The Fight of My Life

By Scott Box

I've always been fascinated by the construction of dams. Humanity has endured dangerous work to either move or contain water throughout history. I deeply respect not only the power of water or the wildness of nature but also the genius God gave humanity to overcome and harness nature. To be clear, I'm not only amazed by the power of water, in this case, the McKenzie River in Oregon State, but by the enormous power and strength of the numerous man-made dams that regulate the river flow. My family has stayed multiple times at a beautiful cabin just a few miles east of the dam along the McKenzie in Leaburg. Being under the dam is a sobering experience. I always think about the ingenuity and engineering required to build and maintain a barrier that holds millions of gallons of water at bay daily.

Interestingly, about 30 miles southwest of that McKenzie River house and Leaburg dam, in Cottage Grove, Oregon, another place exists on a local fork of another Oregon river, the Willamette River. This house on the Willamette could not have existed in that location a hundred years ago had a wealthy lumber baron not literally moved the river out of the way. I don't know any more details; I don't need to! What I do know is that the enterprising man knew where he wanted to build his house. So, rather than adjust his plans to fit the geography, he got a bunch of other rough men to help him move the geography to suit his needs. I find that incredible, fascinating, and maybe a little absurd. Okay, perhaps what that man accomplished is very absurd.

Sure, maybe there was some other sensible reason the lumber baron moved a river to build a dream house. But something tells me he didn't need another reason. Certainly, artificially moving a river goes against all kinds of modern sensitivities. But I'm not that sensitive of a guy, so there is no denying that there is nearly every manner of something romantic and legendary in a tale like this. I love it. This man altered the course of the river to build his dream house. Because - why not? I've visited and stayed a night in that house alongside the Willamette River with my wife, Kariann. A swan lives in the lake in the front yard. Figures, huh?

I have managed bipolar disorder for 16 years. Along the way, I have occasionally considered or reflected on all the "earthworks" I needed to construct to live a healthy, altered life. But unlike the lumber baron who chose to move a river, I had to navigate a bipolar diagnosis. My diagnosis created a flood that caused the river of my life to spill over its banks. I moved immense mental, physical and spiritual "water, dirt and rock" to reveal the proper ground God designed me to cultivate in my life. Uncovering that foundational building spot was unbelievably hard work, but I wasn't building a dream house. Instead, I was fighting for my life.

What I mean when I say "fighting for my life" is that the necessity of maintaining those earthworks felt like a crushing weight to overcome. At the beginning of my bipolar adventure, I thought I was constantly plugging numerous leaks with multiple parts of my body, all at once; all the while, I was begging (screaming) for help (or forgiveness) from others. It was immensely humbling. No, it went beyond humbling and often into disgraceful humiliation. There were countless times when the power of the river (my bipolar and life circumstances) busted right through the embankments I felt so proud I had constructed.

Life wasn't just brutal for me; it was also costly for my family and friends. I imagine that no one could escape receiving damage when the water broke. I picture us sprawled out, sputtering water from our lungs, lying in thick mud and heavy river rock pools. Even if I didn't immediately feel guilty, I eventually did. Occasionally, I felt debilitating shame. I felt shameful because the breaches in the foundation work were directly related to how high my mania took me or how low my depression hauled me. It would take me days or months to feel like I had rebuilt what the waters had washed away. I felt as though I had lost so much time. I was losing hope.

Unlike the lumber baron, who could move the river and then build his dream house on dry land, I was making my foundation in the same place the river continued to flow before it was entirely and finally moved. I hope you can picture the difference I'm trying to communicate. That's just the way mental disabilities like bipolar affect real life. I had to build and move a river at the same time. To be clear, there is no way I could have achieved what I have attained or learned what I have learned or enjoyed despite my fear and brokenness without a Hero to save me. You see, the heavy lifting I was constantly doing to build my beautiful new permanent residence made me incredibly resilient. Jesus Christ, the Great Hero, was my strength. I found strength I didn't know was available to me. Because of Jesus' sacrifice and triumph over death, neither my victories and defeats nor my heroism and villainy could remove my hopeful and necessary desperation for my Great Hero.

Today, I don't have a house below a dam or a mansion in an old riverbed; I have a powerful story, an eternal witness, about how my Savior, Jesus Christ, the Great Hero, rescued me from a bipolar disorder torrent. I will tell my story to tell His story forever.

I thank God for dams and lumber barons.

Reflection with Gina:

> "And He said, 'Your name shall no longer be called Jacob, but Israel; for you have struggled with God and with men, and have prevailed.'"
>
> —Genesis 32:28 (NKJV)

How many of us find echoes of our own lives in Jacob's story? Jacob was about to be reunited with Esau, his brother, from whom he had stolen his birthright and blessing. He isolated himself at the ford of Jabbok and began to battle with God Himself. Jacob refused to release Him without receiving a blessing. He was given a new name, Israel, and also with a physical reminder of the encounter: a dislocated hip.

Can we see ourselves in Jacob's perseverance and transformation? I certainly can. My life has been full of numerous challenges. Each scar is a reminder of what I have been through and how God was there all along. Some might see scars as disfigurements, symbols of vulnerability or weakness, I perceive them as marks of beauty and strength. They are the proof of our resilience, the stories of our encounters with God, and the evidence of our personal growth. Just as Jacob carried his limp as a badge of his spiritual encounter and growth, our scars can serve as powerful reminders of our capacity to overcome adversity and to emerge stronger, more aligned with our purpose and closer to God.

Questions:

1. What path in your life have you seen God reroute and rebuild to where you are today?

2. What are the scars you carry with you?

3. How have you seen God use the scars you carry to help guide others to Him?

Prayer:

God, we are thankful for our scars. They are the evidence of a hard fought journey. Although they are not always wanted or well received, they remind us of how You carried us through difficulties. We open our hands and ask You to use the scars, the winding journey and the dislocated hips in our own story to bring people to the full knowledge of our merciful, gracious and loving God. Thank you for the healing You do in each of our lives everyday in Jesus's name, Amen.

"And He said, 'Your name shall no longer be called Jacob, but Israel; for you have struggled with God and with men, and have prevailed.'"

GENESIS 32:28
(NKJV)

Chapter 4

The Mind of Christ

by Kim Gentry Meyer

The brightness of my sweet childhood began to slowly dim as I reached middle school. That is the first recollection I have of struggling with what I now recognize was depression. I mainly kept my struggle to myself because depression wasn't discussed as openly as it is now. When it was talked about, it was either brushed off as not being a real thing or identified only in its most extreme form. I found the typical response to be, "suck it up," insinuating that I was just being a wimp. So I learned to just keep my mouth shut about it, all the while wondering what was wrong with me.

I remember it as layers of intermittent sadness weaving throughout my days and nights like a shifting tapestry. When it was present, it wove through happy mornings under the Christmas tree, through fun shopping trips with my friends, and at night as I lay in bed listening to the traffic outside my window. Although it was never totally debilitating, it just made everything harder. It made being alone with my thoughts something to avoid. It also made me sad, even when I was happy.

While I was struggling internally, I excelled academically, was musically gifted and was involved in many activities. I was known to be outgoing and upbeat. I had solid friendships. I enjoyed good relationships with my wonderful family. I was not someone who appeared to be depressed. But I struggled. I battled. I answered my own question of what was wrong with me with the assumption that it must be a character weakness to overcome.

Fast-forward to high school, college, grad school, and working as a young professional. It was all more of the same—still high-achieving and still fighting all on my own. Ignoring it, retreating in it, pushing through it, carrying it like a boulder on my back, all while maintaining a growing career and navigating the nuances of adult life. It was a happy life and a blessed life, honestly. But it was also a hard life due to depression.

I eventually landed on an antidepressant that I tolerated well enough to take regularly, which has helped address the physiological aspects of my depression. Medication and counseling peeled away some of the layers of darkness. But there was still a missing piece of the puzzle.

It might sound ridiculous that it took me this long to lean on my faith, considering I have been a practicing Christian all my life. I always tended to keep my struggle with depression hidden away from my faith life because, in my experience, there is still a stigma in the Christian community when it comes to depression. People think you should not be depressed if you are a Christian, or that you should have been healed of it already, or that you are certainly demonized and it is your own fault. This stigma causes shame to rise and silences those who need help the most; at least, that has been my experience. I felt ashamed bringing this "weakness" to the Lord, and I felt guilty complaining to Him because He had already blessed me with a wonderful life. That should be enough. This was my internal narrative for many years, fueled by "the church" and my own self-criticism.

I've found this missing piece over the past couple of years as I've added an intentional spiritual component to my battle with depression. I absolutely believe God heals, and I believe He can heal me completely. I believe there is a spiritual warfare component to depression. We have authority over the spirit of depression in Jesus's name, and I claim that. But for me, freedom from depression has not been a quick fix or a one-size-fits-all prayer formula, even though it often seems that is what the Christian culture demands. Instead, it's been a journey that has included addressing my serotonin imbalance, talking openly with my counselor, and, most recently, renewing my mind in Christ.

This practice of renewing my mind in Christ has been an incredibly effective weapon in my battle with depression. It started when I began to grasp a deeper revelation of Romans 8:6, "The mind governed by the flesh is death, but the mind governed by the Spirit is life and peace." I clumsily began asking the Lord each day to renew my mind, and then I would list out all the things that were bothering me. I have learned over time to talk to Him about even the tiny things that seem insignificant because those tiny things can become bigger and cause problems if not addressed. By taking my problems to Him through prayer and quiet listening and by spending time in His Word daily, I have more peace. Slowly, over time, that peace is crowding out the depression.

I don't pretend my struggle is over, but I can honestly say I'm walking in the greatest freedom I've ever known. That freedom continues to grow as I set a course in one direction: toward the Light. Every day that I lean on renewal through Christ, I move closer and closer toward that Light.

I leave you with the lyrics to a song I wrote to document my battle with depression and the hope I've found in renewing my mind in Christ. May it encourage you in your own journey.

Mind of Christ

by Kim Gentry Meyer and Karl Anderson

Verse 1

I'm overwhelmed

In a world that's not for me

So hard to stay up

When my thoughts take me deep

It's like walking in a dark room

In the middle of the night

Feeling lost and lonely

Cause I can't find the lights

Chorus

I need the mind of Christ to come and cover me

I need the mind of Christ to come and set me free

This battle that I'm facing

Is not the earthly kind

Jesus come restore my peace of mind

Verse 2

I'm holding on

To the Truth I know is real

Who I am

Is more than how I feel

It's like waiting for the summer
In the middle of the snow
The cold feels like forever
But in springtime it goes

Bridge
The mind of the Spirit is life and peace
Darkness has no place in what the Son sets free
©2023 Kim Gentry Music

Reflection with Gina:

> "Now the mindset of the flesh is death, but the mindset of the Spirit is life and peace."
>
> —Romans 8:6 (CSB)

I don't know about you, but Romans 8 is one of my favorite chapters in the entire Bible. When I first started my journey with Jesus, I highlighted, underlined, and memorized the entire chapter. Each verse is not only filled with beautiful reminders but also ignites our spirits, making us want to shout, "Hallelujah!" It begins with the powerful declaration, "There is no condemnation for those in Christ Jesus" (Romans 8:1). Throughout the chapter, our relationship and status with God, secured through Jesus' sacrifice on the cross, are revealed in every verse. A central theme in this chapter is the importance of our mindset.

Each morning and evening, we have the opportunity to release the mindsets of the flesh, allowing us to soak in the Word of God. Dying to our flesh daily creates more space for the Holy Spirit to fill us to overflowing, enabling us to share His goodness, mercy, and grace with others. I love how Kim's song helps us to begin this process, putting us in the right place to start each day with a renewed mind and heart.

Questions:

1. Where has my mind been focused more on lately, the flesh or the Spirit? (be honest)

2. What is holding me back from walking fully in what God has called me to do and be?

3. What practices can I do every day and evening to begin to develop the mind of Christ and what tools do I need, besides the Bible, to do this?

Prayer:

God, I am so grateful for the cross of Christ that gives me a direct line to You through Your Spirit. I repent that my mind has not been focused on you and so neither has other parts of my life. I ask for Your Spirit to wash over me and fill me to overflowing. Remind me to begin and end every day by inviting You in and closing it out while thanking You for what You've done. I open my mind to You, God, and want to know You better. In Jesus's name, Amen.

"Now the mindset of the flesh is death, but the mindset of the Spirit is life and peace."

ROMANS 8:6
(CSB)

Chapter 5

Symbols of Hope

by Cally Logan

Symbols can often convey a message far louder than a lengthy soap box speech ever could. Occasionally, I will be at a coffee shop and reach for my steaming cup of black coffee with two creams when I am met with a glance from eyes whispering vulnerably, "You too?" The symbol on my wrist is a semi-colon tattoo and it represents the sentiment of what could have been the end, but it was not. In other words, the story goes on. It's an unspoken understanding for those who have faced the demon that bellows thoughts and ideas of a permanent ending, but they live on to tell the tale of how their story isn't over yet.

Suicide is not a comfortable subject matter to discuss. The world feels far more at ease with a veneer of shiny, happy people. But when we peel back the surface of that plastic coding, what is underneath is the ability to authentically share with one another and perhaps help someone struggling with how to find real hope.

In my early twenties, I suffered from some pretty deep bouts of depression. I was a college student struggling to keep my grades up while combating several health issues. I knew God and I had a relationship with

Him, but I was not yet at a place where I had really surrendered to God in every area of my life. Call it stubborn youthful pride, or call it petulant ignorance, I thought writing my own story would yield a happily ever after, but it did not. I had this incessant belief that somehow if I could keep myself occupied enough, I would not have to face the reality of how hopeless I felt. Perhaps I could write my own little miracle: a miracle where my health issues were resolved, where I got the prince of my daydreams, and where everything in my life just would work out. It seemed the harder I attempted to control situations, the further to the end of myself I came.

It was Christmas time, and once again, I found myself single, lonely, and unfulfilled in the aspirations I was chasing after like a feather in the wind. It seemed the pen of my own hand had run out of ink, and what was left around me was emptiness, sorrow, despair, and little hope for how anything could turn around. Yet it was at that moment of coming to the end of myself that I finally looked up and realized the One who could satisfy me was there all along; I just hadn't taken the time to notice Christ. So that very night, I threw away the bottle of Tylenol that I had considered guzzling down, and I prayed a simple prayer asking Him to lead my life, direct my steps, and write my story. I surrendered.

A verse that anchored me a lot during this time was Proverbs 3:5–6, "Trust in the LORD with all of your heart, and lean not on your own understanding, but in every way look to Him and He will make your path straight." I had been doing everything the wrong way. I felt it fell upon me to write my own story, trust in myself, and find glory when, in fact, my heart was not where answers were to be found at all. Instead, it was in my coming to know the Maker of my heart. That is how answers were found and paths were laid out, and it was where the mystery of not knowing every facet of everything in my life was met with peace. In coming to know Him, I found true joy and satisfaction.

Years later, I once again faced the demon who suggested endings as a method of escape, but this time, I handled the situation differently. I had endured a traumatic sexual assault that my memory had blacked out in order to cope mentally, only for it to be unearthed years later. I wanted to crawl outside of my own skin because I felt so imprisoned by the haunting of such a horrific event. That familiar voice came slithering back to place the thought of bowing out to find release. During this time, I played the movie *Castaway*[1] on repeat. Like the main character, Chuck, I found myself trapped on a lonely island, unable to escape. In the film, he is met by the pernicious idea that the only escape is death. Yet there was a greater voice telling him not to give in, and one day, a sail would come. What proved true in the movie for Chuck Noland proved true for me as well in a sail coming forward in due time. I came to God vulnerably with my questions, my confusion, my tender and aching spirit, and my pain. He met me with love, compassion, and healing as only a Healer can. He sent a sail through His love, silencing that demon yet again.

So, each time I meet the eyes of someone who makes a pointed glance at my tattoo, those eyes convey a whimper of "Someone understands." I graciously thank God that, indeed, someone understands. God understands and God can heal even the deepest of wounds. Whatever we face, whatever we endure, and whatever we feel imprisoned by will not defeat us, but we must surrender to Him. God holds the key to true freedom, release, healing, and joy. Is He not worthy of our trust, even when we cannot see?

---

1. Zemeckis, R. (Director). (2000). *Cast Away* [Film]. 20th Century Fox

Reflection with Gina:

> "Trust in the LORD with all of your heart, and do not lean on your own understanding; in all your ways know him and he will make your path straight."
>
> —Proverbs 3:5–6 (CSB)

This is a verse most people become familiar with once they become a Christian or go through situations they do not understand. I don't know about you, but this describes how I have felt in so many situations. When we are living on this earth, our finite minds cannot even begin to understand our infinite God. When we lose someone, especially under terrible circumstances, it is so easy to become mad at God and to walk away from Him. Even Jesus got upset about the situation he was experiencing. When he was at Gethsemane, He prayed so hard that He was bleeding. He knew His reason for coming to earth, but even He asked God to take His suffering away: "Father, if you are willing, remove this cup from me. Nevertheless, not my will, but yours, be done" (John 22:42 ESV).

In the last ten years or so, I have learned to run toward Him. This doesn't mean I don't get angry or have all the answers; it just means I have learned that running toward Him is so much better than running away. Cally talks about how she felt so depressed to the point of contemplating taking her own life, to which I can relate. It was at that time that she discovered the hope and security she could find in God in an uncertain world.

God understands every emotion and feeling we have; He created them. The place to begin is to ask Him. Go to Him earnestly and honestly and begin the process of open communication. You may not hear Him audibly, but go to His Word and hear His voice in there.

Questions:

1. What is the area in your life that has led you to question God the most?

2. Is your tendency to run away or to run closer to Him? Why?

3. In what ways can you start or continue the process of open communication with God, especially in moments when life feels overwhelming?

Prayer:

God, I don't understand why bad things happen in this world. Don't You have the ability to change things and take them away? I am so tired of running and being stuck in the same old patterns. I want to run to You, not away, but I don't know if I can. I open my hands, my heart and my mind to You and ask You to help me. I know I will not be able to understand a lot of things on this side of heaven, but I want to trust more in You. Lead my life from this time forward and reveal Yourself to me more and more with each day through Your Word. In Jesus's name, Amen.

"You will keep the mind that is dependent on you in perfect peace, for it is trusting in you. Trust in the Lord forever, because in the Lord, the Lord himself is an everlasting rock!"

ISAIAH 26:3-4
(CSB)

Chapter 6

Living and Active Help

by Wendy Blight

"Where can I go from your Spirit? Where can I flee from your presence? If I go up to the heavens, you are there; if I make my bed in the depths, you are there. If I rise on the wings of the dawn, if I settle on the far side of the sea, even there your hand will guide me, your right hand will hold me fast."
—Psalm 139:7–10 (NIV)

For months, I suffered with unsettledness I couldn't explain. Because my body never recalibrated back to normal, my unsettledness led to anxiety that eventually hijacked my life.

During those months, I experienced escalating symptoms of dizziness, shaking, aches and pains throughout my body. I had no appetite. I couldn't sleep. I suffered from severe panic attacks. Thoughts of never getting better and never experiencing peace again overwhelmed me to the point I wouldn't leave my house, even to make a grocery trip. It felt like the aisles were closing in on me.

In the meantime, I did all the Christian things I knew to do. I reminded myself of the truths I knew. I'm a child of God, an overcomer, loved and seen by God. But they were just words on a page. Empty words. I wasn't walking in them. I didn't believe them. Instead, I felt totally alone and abandoned by God.

What hurt the most was how ashamed I felt. Ashamed because I'm a Bible teacher and Christian speaker. I'm on staff with a women's ministry. I've written books to help women overcome trials in their lives, yet I couldn't overcome my own. I felt like an imposter.

It was the loneliest, darkest place. One night, feeling utterly defeated, helpless and hopeless, I cried and confessed, through tears, these four words.

"Father, I need help."

I knew I needed help to navigate this hard place. So, first, I began counseling. It was the best decision I made because my counselor spoke hard but necessary words that stepped on my toes, *"Wendy, if God isn't changing your circumstances, He has something for you in them."* These words were really hard to hear but even harder to accept. I was so desperate to know if God had something for me in this painful place and I wanted to discover it. I knew the only way to do that was to sit alone with God and listen. This led me to what I call "be still" time. Every night around 9:00 p.m., I committed to sit alone with my Bible, my journal and God. I faithfully stopped what I was doing for my sacred pauses with Jesus.

It was there in that sacred space that God shifted something deep within me. Over time, He ministered to my soul. He placed verses and passages of Scripture before me that brought deep and abiding peace and healing. One of my favorite times with the Lord took to me a psalm with which I was very familiar. As we know from Hebrews 4:12, God's Word is living and active. It speaks a fresh word each time we open it. That's what I encountered that day! I read every word over and over again, begging for God to make it come alive in my heart. In one of those readings, something shifted deep within me. Warmth penetrated my overwhelmed, unsettled, weary soul in ways I couldn't have imagined.

Friend, will you step away for a moment, grab your Bible and read Psalm 139? After you've done that, bring your overwhelmed heart and your limping faith back here because I have beautiful truths and promises I want to share with you.

God knows your every thought, your every emotion, your every decision. (Psalm 139:2)

God goes behind you and ahead of you. There's never a time He's not with you and His eyes aren't upon you. (Psalm 34:15, 139:7–10)

You are alive because God chose to give you life. (Psalm 139:13, 15–16)

You have value and worth simply because your Abba Father created you. You are fearfully and wonderfully made in His image! (Psalm 139:14)

He knit you together in your mother's womb and scheduled each day of your life before you took a single breath. (Psalm 139:15–16)

You have significance because God knows you by name and calls you His beloved son or daughter. (Psalm 139:16, John 10:3)

In the midst of your doubt and hurt, **know these truths.**

- God loves you.

- He grieves when you suffer.

- He runs to you when you're hurting.

- He is with you always.

The best evidence of these promises is Jesus! Read verses 8 and 9 again. I don't think it's an accident that the image David (the author of Psalm 139) paints in verses 8 and 9 is a cross. The cross is the perfect picture of God's lavish, everlasting, unconditional love.

In the midst of your pain, doubt, anxiety, grief, hurt and fear, may you hear today that God loves you unconditionally. Absolutely nothing can change that truth. It's impossible to get beyond His reach. Open your heart to Him. Give God a chance. Commit to "be still" times with Him. Schedule your first sacred pause with Him. Meet Him in Psalm 139. Pray through these truths. He will guide you back into the assurance of His love and give you increased measures of His presence and His deep and abiding peace.

Reflection with Gina:

> "You will keep the mind that is dependent on you in perfect peace, for it is trusting in you. Trust in the Lord forever, because in the Lord, the Lord himself is an everlasting rock!"
> —Isaiah 26:3-4 (CSB)

Who could use more peace? Peace is something that seems to be getting more and more difficult to find here at this point in time. This verse, along with Wendy's story, reminds us that God created each one of us for a special purpose at this specific time in history. None of the things that are going on in the world around us are surprising to God. He has known about it since the beginning of time. The Bible is His way of guiding us in every part of our lives. It is not meant to be a coaster, something collecting dust on a shelf, or even the table leg holder for a broken table. It is living water and bread for our souls. It is truly the only thing that will bring us the perfect peace Isaiah talks about in these verses.

God is truly the only One who can lead and guide you through not only the struggles around you but also the struggles within you. Knowing who you are in Christ will keep you anchored to him no matter what is going on. I am so glad Wendy talked in great detail about Psalm 139. If you didn't before, go and look up those verses and really meditate on them. Then truly ask God to reveal to you the areas where you need His perfect peace to show up in your life. Begin to renew your mind by reading His Word every day and watch what He will do!

Questions:

1. Who is God to you? What is your identity in Him?

2. In what areas of my life could I use more peace? Where am I unsettled?

3. During the craziness of my life, in what ways can I seek out and gain this perfect peace?

Prayer:

God, I am struggling with my identity. I know what the world around me says about me and about what my past has dictated, but I need to know what You say about me. I need to learn from You and discover this perfect peace Your Word describes. I want to trust everything You have said. Reveal to me through the renewing of my mind how I can have peace and not let what is going on around me drag me down. In Jesus's name, Amen.

"You will keep the mind that is dependent on you in perfect peace, for it is trusting in you. Trust in the Lord forever, because in the Lord, the Lord himself is an everlasting rock!"

ISAIAH 26:3-4
(CSB)

SECTION 2

GRIEF AND LOSS

Grief is one of those subjects that no one understands or wants to deal with it or a little bit of both. We have all experienced some form of loss or death of a person, dream, relationship, or other things that you are yelling at the page right now. God never promised us an easy life here on Earth, but He did always promise to never leave or forsake us during those difficult times. As you read the following chapters and listen to the corresponding podcast episodes, I pray you will find hope and begin the process of healing you need to move forward in this beautiful life you have been given. Remember, even though there seems to be no hope after the specific loss, begin by seeking the One who loves you and created you. He will lead you through your journey.

Chapter 7

Empty Arms, Full Heart

by Gina Fox

I had issues with my menstrual cycles since I was 12 years old. This is probably not the type of sentence everyone wants to read at the beginning of a chapter, but stick with me. I was placed on birth control at that age to help regulate everything and was on it until I was 24 years old. I was taken off of them after finding out I had a blood disorder, which I was tested for after my mom ended up with a nine-inch blood clot in the jugular vein in her neck. This blood disorder, MTHFR677T, was something they were just learning about back in 2003–2004 when I discovered I had it. No one really understood much about it at the time. Great—something else for my family to handle! So, for the next ten years, I had struggles with painful, irregular and heavy cycles.

In 2010, I had been off birth control for many years and never got pregnant. My husband, Matthew and I started down a journey of talking with my doctor and even seeing a fertility specialist. I learned I had endometriosis and had at least four procedures during the next four years to remove the buildup happening in my uterus. We did the shots, which were fantastic, let me tell you! We did daily ultrasounds when I was ovulating. We also measured my body temperature and did all the things to try and conceive, yet it never happened. This got to be very expensive because nothing was covered under my insurance plan at the time. So, we stopped all the extra medications and procedures.

Around 2013, my cycles were so unbelievably painful. If I hit my abdomen on the edge of the table or a chair, it felt like someone was punching me repeatedly. Then, I had an incident at work where I was doing an IV on a patient, and he punched me as hard as he could right in the lower abdomen. We weren't sure if I could have been pregnant, so they sent me down to the emergency room and I wasn't, but the doctor ran 50 million other tests. But that is a totally different story. I began to have really tough discussions with my doctor about just how much pain I was in each month. We had done everything we could do by this point between the procedures and medications, and I was at the end of my rope. We discussed another procedure called a uterine ablation. She told me that getting pregnant after having this procedure could lead to some negative effects. I was sad to hear that, but by this point, I just wanted the pain to stop. So, in December, I had the procedure.

But by early 2014, the pain was back just as bad, if not worse than before. I finally said, "I'm done," and the partial hysterectomy was scheduled. This was one of the most difficult decisions I had ever made because this decision was going to end my chances of getting pregnant and end the dream my husband and I had of having our own baby. We had both always wanted to have a daughter and name her Amber. We were devastated, and each of us has had to walk out our grief at different points in our lives since April 2014.

Even though that was the most difficult decision, in some ways, it was the easiest because the pain was instantly gone. It turned out I had adenomyosis, which is a condition where the uterus is enlarged at the lower level. This explained why I was in so much pain and why I was never able to get pregnant. Several years later, I had my ovaries removed after developing multiple cysts over and over again. Since I had the blood disorder, I am unable to be on hormone replacements. I have only gotten through menopause with the help of God and electric fans!

At the time I am writing this, it has been ten years since I have had the procedure. I am sharing my story because I know I am not the only one who has gone through this. My story of infertility doesn't come with a happy ending. There wasn't a baby placed in my arms after a winning battle. My arms are still empty. My womb is gone without any child ever occupying it.

But God. He knew my story before I was even thought of by my parents. I have gone through every stage with God, from being sad, to angry, to hating Him and also hating everyone around me who seemed to get pregnant just by getting sneezed on, to finally accepting my situation. He was able to withstand all of it and keep me in the comfort of His wings. His love and grace are bigger than anything I have experienced and this is the same for you.

Certain times of the year, like Mother's and Father's Day, still hurt like hell, and some years, I cannot even step in the church doors on those days. I am here to say it's okay if you feel that way, too. It is okay to not be okay. If you are reading this, then know that God sees you and He is sitting with you in the suffering. He will guide you and help you lean on your community because we all need each other.

Reflection with Gina:

> *"And we know that all things work together for good to those who love God, to those who are the called according His purpose."*
>
> —Romans 8:28 (NKJV)

This verse was an extremely difficult one for me to wrap my head around when I was going through my infertility journey. I have been a Christian since 1996, although I started going back to church in 2014. As I wrote in the chapter, I was so angry with God and with others. I couldn't understand why everyone else got pregnant so easily and so often, and I couldn't even get pregnant once, not even an "oops." It broke me in so many ways that I almost walked away from God again. Every time I read in Scripture how a woman was barren and then God "opened" her womb. Why not me? I groaned out to God over and over again as Paul said in the verses before the above verse.

As my journey with God continued, I began to understand a little more about why this happened, or at least what I could do about it. I know now that I can have an impact on those around me, especially the children. I am so fortunate to have so many children around me at every age. My brother and sister-in-law have five boys, ranging from ages 11-23, with whom I get to spend time. Also, my friends have kids of a variety of ages with whom I get to spend lots of time. Getting to spend time with and have influence on children decreases the heartache of not having my own. It has been and will continue to be a learning process, but I am so grateful to see how God has truly worked something out and given me more than I could have ever imagined.

Questions:

1. When you read Romans 8:28, what is one thing you question God about the validity of the verse? (Yes, it is okay to question Him. He welcomes your questions!)

2. When you look back at your life, can you see how this verse has applied to you? In what ways? If not, why not?

Prayer:

God, I do not claim to know why things happen the way they do or why You allow certain things to happen. In Your Word, You promise that all things work together for the good of those who are called according to Your purpose. Show me how this is true. Give me revelation in the areas where I have doubts. Lead me to the truth of Your love and Your plan for my life. Lead me down the path of trusting You more and more. In Jesus's name, Amen.

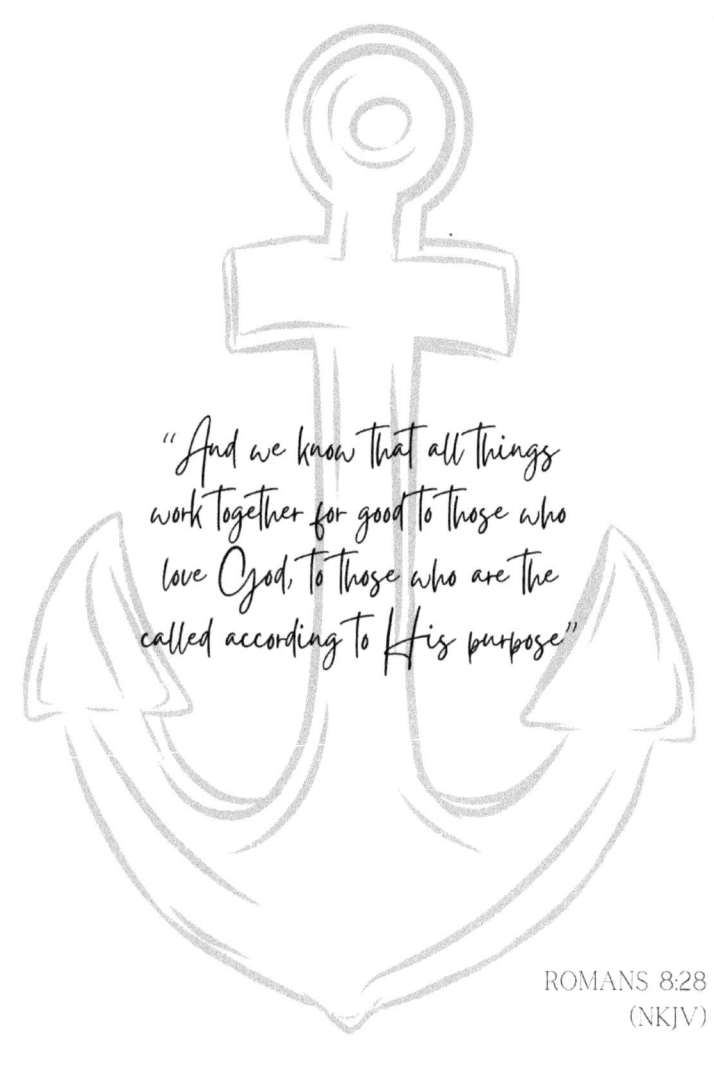

"And we know that all things work together for good to those who love God, to those who are the called according to His purpose."

ROMANS 8:28
(NKJV)

Chapter 8

I Surrender All

by Grace Klein

"I Surrender All" is a beautiful hymn that you may have sung if you've been in church for any amount of time. For those not familiar, the words are sung as a heartfelt declaration to the Lord, expressing love and devotion to Him.

"All to Jesus I surrender
All to Him I freely give
I will ever love and trust Him
In His presence daily live."

It's a moving song that brings a sense of connection with the Lord. The challenge is when it comes to actually living it out. What happens when the Lord asks you to surrender the dream for which you have been hoping or to release the thing you hold closest to your heart? We think, "Anything but that! There's no way I can surrender that!" "You can't expect me to surrender my dream to get married, have a baby, and start a family. I can't release my career and future to you. That's just too much to ask." The reality is that it's a lot easier to sing "I Surrender All" than to actually surrender all. We tend to have an easier time surrendering *some* things rather than *all* things, especially when it comes to our hopes, dreams, desires and possessions.

I experienced that several years ago when I realized I needed to surrender the dream of birthing children. For months, I'd been experiencing painful cramps, heavy bleeding, pressure, bloating, and constantly needing to urinate. I recognized the symptoms from something I'd experienced over ten years ago, but I didn't want to face the fact I could possibly be going through the same situation again. I went to see my OB-GYN and she confirmed my fears: my symptoms were due to a large number of benign tumors, called fibroids, in my uterus.

"*Not again!*" I groaned.

I'd had an abdominal myomectomy ten years ago to have 21 fibroids removed and they had been replaced by new ones that were impacting every aspect of my life. She explained that I was at the equivalent of being five months pregnant, and the largest fibroid was pressing on my bladder, resulting in me constantly having to urinate. While I could deal with the weight gain, painful cramps and heavy bleeding each month, it was the never-ending need to use the bathroom that wrecked me. What started as waking up once in the middle of the night to go to the bathroom turned into an endless season of sitting on my toilet instead of sleeping through the night.

She said, "I can remove the fibroids as a temporary solution, but because you are still young, they will likely grow back again. The only way to get rid of them permanently is to do a hysterectomy."

"Nooo!" I cried out in disbelief. "There has to be some other option! That can't be the solution!"

My chest began to heave and tears welled up in my eyes as I realized what this would mean. My childhood dream of birthing children was shattered. I would not hold a baby in my arms while my husband carried our toddler.

As reality set in, my tears turned to anger. "Why is this happening to me? God, why aren't You doing something?" I fumed. I was terrified at the thought of removing something from my body that, to me, was the very essence of womanhood. Would I someday regret this permanent decision to remove the ability to create a human being, raise a child and leave a legacy?

I could not sleep in the weeks leading up to the procedure. I resented that God had not healed me, especially when the first instruction He gave Adam and Eve was to "be fruitful and multiply" (Genesis 1:28 NLT). Instead of experiencing the beauty of carrying a child, I was carrying fibroids.

The "H" day eventually came. By that point, my anger had subsided and I had made peace with the fact that my uterus needed to be removed. I would have preferred God to heal me, but I recognized that His ways are higher than my own. On the way to the surgery, I sensed the Lord ask me:

"Grace, when did you give Me your life?"

"When I was a little girl," I replied.

He continued: "Did that include your uterus?"

I paused as I thought about when I'd surrendered my life to Jesus. I'd figured it would involve living for Him and loving others, *not* relinquishing my uterus. As Christians, when we talk about surrendering to the Lord, we often refer to our careers, our future, our plans, or our finances. I'd never heard anyone mention their uterus. But in that moment, I realized that when I surrendered my life to the Lord, it meant all of me, including my uterus.

So, after a lengthy pause, I slowly answered, "Yes."

I didn't know how the decision was going to affect me, but I knew that the Lord was with me and I could trust Him. I cupped my hands over my abdomen and felt the hard lump. Taking a deep breath, I uttered words I never thought I would ever say. "Lord, this is not what I pictured for my uterus." I sighed heavily. "But I surrender all of me, including my uterus, to You. I believe that through it, You are going to birth more in the spiritual than I would in the natural." Although everything in me did not want to let go of this special organ in my body, I felt an unexplainable peace in releasing it into the hands of the One who had created it.

Surrendering something is never easy. But I have come to find that there is a special intimacy we experience with the Lord that comes through surrender. We see that in the life of Christ. Jesus surrendered His life on the cross, and through His death and resurrection, we have the promise of eternal life with the Father. His ultimate surrender allows us to have an intimate relationship with God. I pray that as you surrender whatever the Lord is calling you to do, you will experience His presence in a deeper way.

Reflection with Gina:

"There was also a prophetess, Anna, a daughter of Phanuel, of the tribe of Asher. She was well along in years, having lived with her husband seven years after her marriage, and was a widow for eighty-four years. She did not leave the temple, serving God night and day with fasting and prayers. At that very moment, she came up and began to thank God and to speak about him to all who were looking forward to the redemption of Jerusalem."

—Luke 2:36–38 (CSB)

In this passage, we are introduced to Anna. She had lost her husband after only seven years together. While the Bible doesn't say that she never had children, we can assume from the passage she did not because it says she was in the temple day and night. She saw Jesus and began to acknowledge who He was in front of everyone who was awaiting the Messiah. People looked to her with high regard because she had spent so much time in the temple, giving God her all.

Grace talked about how painful it was walking through infertility, but when God asked her, "Grace, when did you give Me your life," she was reminded of how when she gave her life to Him, it was in every area. We all have had to go through something that made us confront this very same question. I am sure as you read this, you remember a time when something bad happened, or you received a diagnosis that you thought would knock you out for good. You may be going through something now and cannot find a way through the pain. For that, I am sorry. But I want to offer you the true hope that comes out of a relationship with God. He has turned the pain that Anna, Grace and I have suffered into a purpose we could have never imagined. If you will give your pain to Him, He will do the same for you.

Questions:

1. What does Anna's devotion to spending day and night in the temple say about her faith and relationship with God?

2. Grace was reminded that giving her life to God meant surrendering every area, including her pain. Have you experienced a moment where you had to surrender something difficult to God? How did that impact your faith?

3. What practical steps can you take to lean into the hope that comes from a relationship with God, especially in times of pain?

Prayer:

God, I don't know how to walk through some of the situations I am experiencing to get closer to You. When I gave my life to You, I didn't fully understand that it meant every part of my life, even the areas over which I still seek control. Help me to fully let go and trust in Your ultimate plan for my life. You see things I don't, so reveal the parts I need to know and trust You with the rest. Help me to have the faith Anna had after she faced not only the loss of her husband but also the loss of her dreams. In Jesus's name, Amen.

"There was also a prophetess, Anna, a daughter of Phanuel, of the tribe of Asher. She was well along in years, having lived with her husband seven years after her marriage, and was a widow for eighty-four years. She did not leave the temple, serving God night and day with fasting and prayers. At that very moment, she came up and began to thank God and to speak about him to all who were looking forward to the redemption of Jerusalem."

LUKE 2:36-38
(CSB)

Chapter 9

Overcoming the Deep Waters

By Amy Joob

Grief sucks! You may be thinking I shouldn't say that word, but if you have recently lost a loved one, there are a few choice words you may have to describe the grief you are processing. Perhaps you have gone through one loss on top of another and it feels like an avalanche is crumbling around you.

I was on an uphill trajectory with the release of my second book. I had won an award, and I was traveling, speaking, and finding my new groove. Then, all of a sudden, my dad fell ill. After two unsuccessful heart procedures, my dad went home to be with Jesus two months later. It felt like I was free-falling. My foundation was rocked to the core. My dad was my biggest supporter and cheerleader. He owned a successful online book and collectible store and shipped his goods all over the world. He owned a warehouse on their property in northern Minnesota that housed over 25,000 volumes of books in addition to countless magazines, comics, antiques, and other collectibles. My dad promoted me through media outlets and interviews, bought and sold books, prayed relentlessly, and encouraged me to keep writing.

Three weeks after my dad passed, our son went away to his first summer camp and was assaulted by another boy. It was a nightmare. The leadership did not stand with us, which resulted in us leaving the church. Then, my mom was moved to assisted living due to her dementia and within a few months, my former sister-in-law and my aunt passed away.

When you lose a loved one or watch a loved one go through debilitating pain, it's difficult to explain to others. Perhaps you can relate to Job, who had and literally lost it all. He experienced one devastation after another as children, livestock, wealth, and all that he held dear were stripped away from him.

What do you do when the bottom falls out? Even through the grief fog, the unexpected loss of my dad, and the horrific betrayal we experienced with our son, I was determined to hold onto my faith during the storm. I tossed, turned, and wept through many sleepless nights. I felt as though I was drowning and endured many panic attacks. I cried out to Jesus and clung to Him as my refuge. He is the one who held me up and kept me from drowning.

Lamentations 3:19–26 (NLT) says,

> "The thought of my suffering and homelessness is bitter beyond words. I will never forget this awful time, as I grieve over my loss. Yet I still dare to hope when I remember this: The faithful love of the Lord never ends! His mercies never cease. Great is his faithfulness; his mercies begin afresh each morning. I say to myself, "The Lord is my inheritance; therefore, I will hope in him!" The Lord is good to those who depend on him, to those who search for him. So it is good to wait quietly for salvation from the Lord."

One night, I dreamed I was alone in a raging storm in dark, choppy waters. I struggled to stay afloat and not be sucked under by the pull of the angry waves. I called out to a man in a boat nearby, but he did not come to help. The captain of the small wooden watercraft could not maneuver near me through the storm. He merely shouted instructions at me and miraculously, I could hear him. The captain pointed me in the direction of a narrow concrete walkway that was just under the surface of the water. In desperation, I called on Jesus to save me. He came instantly, smiled warmly, picked me up, and ushered me to the concrete walkway. He showed me a solid place to stand on so I would not drown in the raging sea and a path on which to move forward in spite of the churning water, pelting rain, and darkness that engulfed me. Jesus showed me the path of life and gave me hope in my moments of deepest despair.

> "When you go through deep waters, I will be with you. When you go through rivers of difficulty, you will not drown. When you walk through the fire of oppression, you will not be burned up; the flames will not consume you."
>
> —Isaiah 43:2 (NLT)

In the midst of this season of grieving, my family was able to get away for a few weeks to Florida. I found solace in the warm sunshine, salty breezes off the ocean, and relaxed rhythm of life. I began to journal, cry, share, and process all the pain, loss, and tragedy that had occurred in just a few short months. I was determined to continue reading through the Bible in a year and began to listen to the scriptures through my YouVersion app. I talked to a couple of trusted friends and contacted my Christian therapist. I gave myself permission to grieve and to go in a new direction as Jesus led my family on the concrete path.

After watching church services online and visiting several churches in our area, we found one to attend. My friend, who also lost her dad and whose son was also assaulted at the camp, told me about Grief Share. We attended together and began to process our pain with a supportive group. With Jesus guiding me and a new group around me, I felt the fog slowly lift. Our son even decided to try the youth service one Sunday morning. We worked with therapists and looked for fresh ways to move forward as a family.

In addition to writing and speaking, I began to pursue certification to become a transformational life coach. I embraced a new chapter in my life. The grief and loss are not the end of my story. I believe God has the final word and I continue to cling to the promise in my life verse, "For I know the plans I have for you," declares the Lord, "plans to prosper you and not to harm you, plans to give you hope and a future" Jeremiah 29:11 (NIV).

Reflection with Gina:

> "But those who trust in the Lord will renew their strength; they will soar on wings like eagles; they will run and not become weary, they walk and not faint."
> —Isaiah 40:31 (CSB)

Grief is a journey that can drain our strength and leave us feeling utterly depleted. In times of loss, it can be difficult to find the energy to face each day, let alone the hope to keep moving forward. Isaiah 40:31 offers a powerful promise to those who are struggling.

This verse speaks directly to our weary hearts. When we place our trust in the Lord, He promises to renew our strength. It's not a strength that comes from within ourselves, but a strength that can only come from Him that lifts us above our circumstances, like eagles soaring in the sky. This doesn't mean that our grief will disappear or that the pain will magically go away. Instead, it means that God will give us the strength to endure and keep moving forward, even when the road is difficult.

In the depths of grief, we may feel as though we are walking through a dark valley with no end in sight. But God assures us that He is with us, renewing our strength day by day. As we trust in Him, we can find the courage to keep walking, even if it's just one step at a time. In time, we will find that we can run again with hearts full of hope and a renewed sense of purpose.

Questions:

1. What does it mean to you to "soar on wings like eagles" in the middle of grief? How can this imagery help you see your situation from a different perspective?

2. Isaiah 40:31 speaks about running and not becoming weary, walking and not fainting. In what ways have you experienced God's sustaining power during your grief journey? How can you rely on Him for renewed strength today?

Prayer:

God, thank You for renewing my strength as I trust in You during this difficult time. I know You will never leave me through not only this time in grief and loss but also the times I know will occur in the future. Whether it is walking through the physical death of someone, the death of a dream, or the death of what we thought our community looked like, I know You are standing with me through it all, holding my hand, wrapping me in Your feathers that comfort me. Jesus, you have experienced every feeling I have because you lost everything and felt the darkness on the cross. Thank you for never leaving me! In Jesus's name, Amen

"But those who trust in the Lord will renew their strength; they will soar on wings like eagles; they will run and not become weary, they walk and not faint"

ISAIAH 40:31
(CSB)

Chapter 10

Taking Authority Over Grief

by Lacy Grace

I began my journey of overcoming grief starting in November of 2021. On November 18, two days before my husband's birthday, his father passed away from COVID-19. During this time, we also found out that my sister-in-law was diagnosed with stage four colon cancer.

The day before my father-in-law's calling hours, my mother was admitted to the hospital with COVID-19. Anyone who knows me knows how close I was to my mom. She was my best friend and we did everything together. My mom was a born-again believer who loved the Lord and her family. While she was in the hospital, she was able to bring two of her roommates to Christ. When my mom's health started to decline, we would ask my mom if she was still fighting. She would nod her head even though she was not able to open her eyes.

I was with my mom every day, all day during visiting hours while she was in the hospital. We would read God's Word, listen to worship music, and pray. At one point, I remember being on my knees in the corner of the room, just praising God. I didn't understand all that was going on, but I made a choice to trust God through it *all*.

While I won't go into the details of our hospital experience, it's important to acknowledge that our interactions with some of the hospital staff were less than ideal, compounding the already heightened emotions we were experiencing. I thank God that I made a choice to walk in love because I did not need anything to hinder my prayers from being answered during this time.

On the morning of December 3, before my mom passed, I had a dream that my mom was sitting in a wheelchair in the hospital room and she was glowing white. As I entered the room, she told me that she was healed. God healed her, and she was coming home. I woke up from this dream, went to the bathroom and returned to bed.

A few moments later, I got a phone call from the hospital to come quickly that my mom was declining. My family and I rushed to the hospital and the nurse was telling me that they wanted to remove my mom from the CPAP (my mom was not on a ventilator), medicate her, and let her pass away. I told them "No" at that moment. When I was able to see my mom, I asked her this question, "Mom! Are you still fighting? I need to know what you want me to do. Are you still fighting?" She shook her head no. I asked her again, and she shook her head again. At that moment, I decided to honor my mom's wishes instead of my own. My heart wanted to make her stay, but I knew she was going to heaven. So, I signed the paperwork to allow them to medicate my mom and remove the CPAP. My mom fought until the very end, when she transitioned to heaven.

We were in a fight with darkness. After making this decision and everything that I went through, the devil tried to use these moments to attack me. After Mom passed, I was being attacked with lies in my thoughts and emotions that said I killed my mom since she did not know what I was asking because of the medications. I thought that if I had waited longer, she would still be here. In reality, I didn't understand all that was going on, but I had made a choice to trust God.

We found out that my dad also had COVID-19 right after my mom went into the hospital. My dad was not doing well and at one point, I thought that my dad might not make it, but **_glory be to God_**, my dad recovered. The day after my mom's funeral, my dad developed some health problems and we had to make some decisions. My mom had just transitioned into heaven and I was with my dad, who was looking to me to make this decision for him.

On Father's Day 2022, we were getting ready to go out with my husband and my dad. My husband got a phone call that his sister was not well and she was going to the hospital. She transitioned to heaven that day.

Then on July 3, 2022, we were getting ready for the celebration of life for my sister-in-law. While I was in the kitchen, I heard my husband say, "I can't do this." I turned around and my husband was on his knees on the floor. I called the ambulance and he was admitted to the hospital for vomiting, dizziness, and the inability to stand on his own. They were not sure what was causing the symptoms because all the tests were coming back with good results. I remember going into the parking lot of the hospital and yelling out, "Satan, you can't have my husband!" My husband was diagnosed with a mini-stroke, but **_our God_** showed up. My husband was released from the hospital two days later and the doctors told him they had never seen anyone recover so quickly. My husband went from where he couldn't stand, use the bathroom, or walk normally to behaving like nothing had happened.

I was still overcoming grief from my loved ones who had recently passed. I was being attacked with difficult thoughts and feelings, but I knew to draw close to God and stand my ground. I was praying in the spirit and declaring the Word of God. I reached out to faith-filled friends to pray. I was very selective on who I asked to pray. I didn't want someone praying that was going to speak death or defeat over the situation. I'm truly thankful for friends who prayed and believed with me.

Grief tries to paralyze you. If you don't process it, it will overtake you. The Bible tells us, "For assuredly, I say to you, whoever says to this mountain, 'Be removed and be cast into the sea,' and does not doubt in his heart, but believes that those things he says will be done, he will have whatever he says. Therefore I say to you, whatever things you ask when you pray, believe that you receive them, and you will have them" Mark 11:23–24 (NKJV).

You *must* speak to your mountain of grief and believe God when you are speaking. The Bible also says in James 4:7 (CSB), "Therefore, submit to God. Resist the devil, and he will flee from you." **You must resist the devil.** James 1:17 (KJV) also tells us, "Every good gift and every perfect gift is from above, and cometh down from the father of lights." Satan will try to bring these thoughts and feelings back because you are free in Christ. When you know where a thought comes from, then you know how to take them captive. When thoughts or feelings come, how do they affect you? Sad? Depressed? Happy? This will help you know where the thoughts are originating. You can apply this to anything you face in life, including divorce, loss of freedom, declining health, or grief.

I could have chosen to hold onto these feelings, have a "poor me" attitude, or think that I was the only one going through it. Instead, I made a choice to fight back and stand my ground, and when I did this, **the devil fled**. When I came to the realization of how real heaven is, and this is not goodbye but "see you later," this changed everything. In the blink of an eye, I will see them again. My mom is living her best life right now and she's more alive now than she has ever been. She's waiting for her loved ones to join her and tell us all about heaven. She has her health and her mansion now. I must complete the work that God has called me to do and I know I will see her when my work is completed. What a joyous day that will be!

Reflection with Gina:

> "Therefore, submit to God. Resist the devil, and he will flee from you."
>
> —James 4:7 (CSB)

When I worked at the hospital, they would do yearly training with us about what to do in case of an active shooter. The basic concept of this training was to teach you the ways to survive the attack. You can either flee (run away) or fight. The first goal was to get out of the situation as fast as possible, so running away was the first option. If that was not possible, then you would fight like hell. You start throwing anything you can get your hands on. You bite, kick, scratch, or punch whatever you can find on the attacker. Another part of the training was being able to quickly analyze your environment, knowing the exits closest to you or where to hide and what can be used as a weapon.

This was to help our brains get wired to be able to survive a potential attack. This same strategy can be used in our spiritual lives. When we are God's children and walking with Him, the enemy will hate us. He will use every tactic he can find to take us out. He will hit us in the areas in which we are weak and the areas that have worked before. Attacks will certainly happen, yet God will help us resist the devil.

In order to defeat the enemy, we need to train. This means spending time in God's Word, prayer, fasting, worship, participating in community, and attending a Bible-believing church. When we do these things consistently, we will recognize what is abnormal and we will know how to react. We will start slinging verses in the devil's direction, reminding him that he has been defeated and he cannot take control of us. Renewing our minds with God's Word will leave less room for the enemy's attacks.

But what does this have to do with grief and loss? It has everything to do with it. This is when we can be at our lowest. Lacy was vulnerable after the loss of her mom, but she remembered very quickly that Jesus overcame death and the grave. Because of this, she will see her mom again in heaven. I was vulnerable when I lost my grandmother, but the Holy Spirit helped me to overcome my darkest time and his influence is the reason I am here today. Resist the attacks of the enemy and remind him that we are overcomers because of Jesus. He needs to leave because he has already been defeated!

Questions:

1. In what ways has the enemy tried to exploit your vulnerabilities during times of grief? Consider how you've felt most attacked when you were grieving or experiencing loss. How did you respond, and what can you do differently in the future?

2. How can you train your mind and spirit to be ready for spiritual attacks? Think about the habits or disciplines you can incorporate into your daily life to strengthen your spiritual defenses. How can these practices help you recognize and resist the devil's schemes?

Prayer:

God, thank you for guiding me through times of grief and loss. Help me to stand firm in my faith, especially when I feel at my weakest. This is the time where the enemy will try to creep in and take everything from me. Draw me deeper into You and train my body, mind, and spirit so that when the attacks come, I will know what to do. Lead me to places in Your Word where others have had to face similar problems and discover how they fought the fight of faith and did not fall away. Bring me into a deeper relationship with You so that there is no room for the devil's antics to get a foothold, even in loss. Comfort those who have walked this walk and are still trying to get out. Let them know they are not alone and are loved by You. In Jesus's name, Amen.

"Therefore, submit to God. Resist the devil, and he will flee from you"

JAMES 4:7
(CSB)

SECTION 3

SURVIVAL

Survival can take many forms. If you watch or are aware of the show Survivor, you see what happens when people are put to the physical, mental, and emotional test of being somewhere they have never been with people they don't know doing things they may never have done before. I don't know about you, but what I have been through in my life is enough "pushing limits" as I can handle! You are a survivor! I have heard it said by many people that you have survived 100% of your worst days, which you have! I bet it was difficult and there were days you didn't feel like you would make it through. You may be feeling that way right now, but let me encourage you with something. Although what you are going through seems too heavy to bear, ask God to take it from you. Hand it over to Him because His yoke is easy and His burden is light (Matthew 11:30 NKJV).

As you read the stories of people who have survived the hills and valleys in their lives, you will gain the hope you need to begin your own journey and know you can make it through!

Chapter 11

Surviving the Hills and Valleys

by Gina Fox

In my dedication to this book, I talked about the impact three different women had on my life. I was not going to go deeper into the story of my life with and losing two of them. But as I was going through the music list for this section, a particular song came on and I began to think about my mom and my grandma and felt as though God was leading me to put this in here. I do not know who this chapter is for, but I know through personal experience that relationships between mothers and daughters can be complicated. I pray that my story will help you in some way, shape, or form to work toward reconciliation, healing, or just being able to see and walk through your own grief and loss in a different way.

My Mother

I was a sick child, but my parents were always there for me when I was in the hospital. They supported everything I did, from ballet to playing tennis. My relationship with my mother really changed during my teenage years. We were able to tolerate each other, even though she was hypercritical of everything I did.

However, as the years went on, we were unable to be in the same room together without a fight breaking out. She began to fight me on every decision I made because they were not what she wanted from me or for me. I began dating my future husband at the age of 20, and she had a lot of judgment toward him and me. I was kicked out of the house less than a month later.

My relationship with my mom was filled with many small hills and huge valleys. There were times when everything would be going okay and then there were times of silence. During the next 12 years, my brother got married, we lost a nephew to leukemia, and four of my nephews were born. Then, in 2010, she came over to my home and said some cruel things about me and my then-fiancee. I told her that I loved her, but she needed to leave my home. That was the last time I ever spoke to her. She passed away at the age of 53 in 2013, after three years of us not speaking.

That was over 11 years ago. There have been a lot of emotions that came with that, including guilt, sadness, anger, and grief. I have had to do a lot of soul-searching to see where I was wrong and what I could have done differently. I decided to write a five-page letter to her that is in her casket. This letter says everything I needed to say, but never got the chance. I wish I had known her time was coming to an end so I could have reconciled with her in person, but I have been able to forgive myself and her over time.

I just went through my eleventh Mother's Day without my mom. There are times that I miss her, and there are times when I mourn the relationship I wish I had with her. I have slowly realized that some of the issues my mother dealt with had nothing to do with me personally but were her own struggles. She had her share of challenges, especially her bipolar disorder, which started before I was even born. When I consider those things, I can give her grace.

My Grandmother

My brother and I spent a lot of time with our grandparents on my dad's side growing up because our parents worked and my mom was always fighting with her parents. My grandmother was someone I looked up to in many different ways and for many different reasons. I gained my love of books, music, movies, crossword puzzles, and of God from her. I remember her having a separate area in her home designated as her place to read or just to be alone. She raised two boys and had a codependent husband, so she needed that space. She and I would take trips to the library together, check out multiple books and just sit and read. Then we would take them back and get more. We would sit and do all kinds of puzzles, whether it was word finds, crosswords, or the ones you needed a table to put together. She would come up to the hospital when I was sick, which was often, and bring me things to do or just sit and watch television with me or watch me sleep.

She was one of the most consistent people in my life. I didn't always appreciate it as a teenager and young adult because I was so involved in my own life and struggles. As the issues with my mom got worse and as I grew older, she became a mom to me. I would call her almost every day when I went to work because she was the only one up that early. That's something I didn't get from her! I began to notice things about her I didn't see as a child. I noticed how she kept her Bible and multiple devotionals on her table. Other than taking care of my grandpa's morning needs, she did not do anything else until she went through them. Also, the books she read when I was young went away and Christian books replaced them. She always went to church on Sunday and volunteered with the women's group no matter which Lutheran church she went to, and she only went to two different ones in her lifetime. She had a calm presence no matter what was happening. I went to her for advice in all aspects of my life. Although she was calm and quiet, she was not afraid to let me know I was being a "little bitty" or to tell Don, my grandpa, to knock it off. She and I were the only ones who could calm my grandpa down, and I have the picture to prove it!

When my mom passed in 2013, she was the one who called me at work to tell me. She was one of the people I truly leaned on during that time. Then in August of 2014, I received a phone call that she was in the emergency room. It was there that my dad and I found out she had cancer. She had three large tumors and I ended up being the one to tell her. I didn't leave her alone at the hospital because she had given me power of attorney years before and wanted me to be involved in every decision she made and to hear everything the doctors were telling her. Being a nurse, I could answer questions and be an interpreter because doctors are not always clear. We found out it was metastatic cancer that began in her colon and had spread everywhere.

During the next nine weeks, I sat with her as she made the decision to go home with hospice, fought to get her the proper care, and even had to fight with her on some days. The roles were reversed. I became everything she was to me growing up. I helped her with her daily needs, shopped for her, and would not leave her side except when she would tell me to do so. The night before she passed away, I was sitting in the chair doing schoolwork for nursing school. All of a sudden, the papers on the refrigerator started swaying and my dog's ears perked up and she started looking around. I had chills and felt something leave the room. I realized it was her spirit leaving her body and that it wouldn't be much longer until her death. The next morning, I went to her apartment on my way to work and helped her with some things. Then I whispered in her ear to wait until I got back. At noon, I got the call from my dad. I left work, called my husband, and got to the apartment. When I walked in, I let out the most guttural noise that I have ever heard myself make, held her, and cried. The next week became a blur, but she had everything prepared and paid for, so I didn't have to worry about anything.

The reason I am putting this in the survival section is because of what happened with their losses and what happened next. The same day I buried my grandmother, I lost a friendship that had been a major part of my life for over 12 years. I was devastated and didn't understand what I did for her to walk away from me. Within the next few weeks, I fell and broke my wrist, had surgery, and couldn't work, yet I finished the internship for my bachelor's degree in nursing and graduated on time. I was so overwhelmed and distraught that one day, I contemplated ending it all. I had a huge meltdown to the point where I was screaming, yelling, and slamming my head on the pillow. I wanted to die. All I would have had to do was go to the dresser drawer and grab the gun and it would have been over. I felt this pressure on top of me that was keeping me on the bed. I did not know it at the time, but the Spirit of the Living God kept me on the bed.

For a few years after that, I prayed for God to give me friends. I wanted not just surface friendships but real and true girlfriends with whom I could do life. I am here to say that He has truly given me abundantly more than I could ask or think. I now have a group of friends that I consider family. Every day, I thank God that in the face of some of my biggest losses, He showed up and showed off the most! He will do the same for you!

Reflection with Gina:

> "Whom have I in heaven but You? And there is none upon earth that I desire besides You. My flesh and my heart fail; But God is the strength of my heart and my portion forever."
> —Psalm 73:25–26 (NKJV)

One day, while she was on hospice, my grandmother asked me to read the Bible to her because she had become so weak that she could no longer do it on her own. I opened the Bible to see where it landed, and I landed on these verses. These would be the final verses we would read together.

Every day of her adult life, she would take care of her husband before he went to work and then she sat on her couch or at her table to do her Bible study. She would make her first cup of coffee and read four or five devotional books and her Bible before she would begin taking care of her children and grandchildren. I am sure there were days when this did not occur or happened at a different time of the day, but she did not like missing church or her study time. When her health began to deteriorate, she could not do this anymore. But I do not doubt that her time in the Word over her entire life sustained her throughout those last weeks and months.

Now, I am not going to sit here and act like I do this every day, but going down memory lane and writing these words reminds me just how important it is to make this a part of my daily life. I pray it does for you, too.

Questions:

1. How has reading about the legacy my grandmother left encouraged you about the importance of spending time with God?

2. What steps will you take to implement spiritual practices into your daily life?

3. When you think about the legacy you want to leave behind, what do you hope is included?

Prayer:

God, I repent of the times I do not include You as part of my day. I know I don't read my Bible or pray and spend time with You as You desire. I truly desire to spend time with You and be in a relationship with You that is better than anything this world can offer. I open myself to You right now and ask for Your help to make our time together not just a routine but something I can't live without. I truly want to serve You with everything I am and with all You have given me. I relinquish control and step out of the way. In Jesus's name, Amen.

"Whom have I in heaven but You? And there is none upon earth that I desire besides You. My flesh and my heart fail; But God is the strength of my heart and my portion forever."

PSALM 73:25-26
(NKJV)

Chapter 12

Surviving Hell to Find Hope

By Brit Eaton

What kind of grown woman goes back to junior high school, literally and figuratively? Well, me. Twenty-seven years since French-rolled jeans, rainbow bangs, and R.E.M. on repeat—a little older and perhaps a little wiser—I consciously chose to go back to the building where it all began...where I nearly lost myself and my life.

Now, they don't just let anyone into school buildings these days. I didn't have to dodge security or call in advance to gain permission for non-parental entry. Here's a little context: At long last, my hometown district got funding for a new junior high school building. Before the old one was demolished, they invited alumni to come walk the hallowed halls one last time.

It made me so happy, and I knew I had to get in on it—not to reminisce or reconnect, but to give a big ol' proverbial middle finger to the seasonal establishment, whoever they were at the time. I hoped to get a front-row seat to the demolition of the original object of my struggles, complete with popcorn and 3-D glasses. Bring on the wrecking ball.

Before you think I'm overreacting, I should let you know that it was in this broken-down building that I first experienced trauma.

Things like bullying, even after I'd turned the other cheek.

Sexual assault, even after I knew "no" meant no.

Spiritual abuse, even at school-sanctioned prayer gatherings.

Gender discrimination, intellectual tear-down, political manipulation, and socioeconomic marginalization.

Yes, even as an upper-middle-class white kid with a ton of privilege.

So I went, ready to burn the place down. But a strange thing happened when I got there. I had a chance to see it all with fresh eyes, the stuff of my present-day nightmares.

The bathrooms in which I spent my lunch crying.

The deep classroom closets where my innocence was taken.

The old and busted golden lockers that made me late and hid my shame.

The classrooms where I couldn't focus and felt I'd never belong.

The central steps I'd collapsed down one day—wondering if life was worth living at the age of 14.

Yes, I had friends. They were good, for the most part. But most of them were hurting as badly as me, so they didn't know how to help. Yes, I had involved parents. They were there for me, one hundred percent. But they couldn't find context for a world they didn't understand. Neither could I.

What about the administrators? They turned a blind eye, or so it felt. To be fair, I don't think they even knew what to look for in 1994—and I certainly didn't know what to ask for, either. They know better now.

But here's what I want you to hear and know with your whole heart: My past, through a healed, whole, Jesus-centered lens, seemed so... small. I walked the halls with my sweet baby sister, my safe person. We marveled at a structure that was once so overwhelming that now had little to no power over me. I named the pain nestled concretely within the water-damaged ceilings, the puke-pink walls, and the creaky 127-year-old wooden steps of what we always called the "red brick." The sights and the smells were all still there. But they had no power.

I gazed solemnly into the same gym locker room mirrors where I was told (and believed) that I would never be enough—physically, emotionally, intellectually, or spiritually. But they had no power.

I sat on those fateful central steps where I'd fallen...the ones that still seemed so ominous in my dreams...and realized how tiny they were in real life. They always were, but I just didn't have eyes to see it. They had no power.

That old building has no power over me anymore. I respect her historical significance, but I was more than ready to let her go, as were hundreds if not thousands of kids who endured her asbestos-laden walls. I'll cling to the lessons she taught me and the life she eventually brought me for a lifetime. God didn't deliver me from her, but he brought me through the struggles I had there.

At 41 years old, I went back to junior high and got reacquainted with my 14-year-old self. For the first time since 1994, I felt true, authentic, honest compassion for her. Sure, she could have been braver, maybe stronger. But she could have also been far more loved.

I can't go back in time and be the person I needed, like someone who would perhaps keep me from attempting suicide six short months later at 15. But I *can* be that person today. I can be one moved with compassion to make a difference in an emerging generation of would-be believers in a good Father God.

For *one* person who needs to know how much their life matters.

For *one person* who has no one to go to and nowhere else to go.

For *one* life that might transform *thousands* of lives long after mine is over.

I'm living proof there is *hope*. I'm still breathing, still searching, and still chasing after God, fully aware and eternally grateful that He was and is with me every step of the journey.

We go through what we go through so we can help others go through what we went through. In time, I hope we can unapologetically remove the systemic spiritual barriers that keep our young kids from complete freedom. They deserve better. I did, too. I know that now. So will my daughter. Thank you, Jesus, for a brand-new life—one I don't deserve. Thank you for healing, grace, forgiveness, and hope.

Reflection with Gina:

> "I sought the Lord, and He answered me and delivered me from all my fears."
>
> —Psalm 34:4 (ESV)

This verse holds a special place in my heart, especially when I reflect on the darkest moments of my life. There were times when fear seemed to overwhelm me and the weight of traumatic events felt like more than I could bear. Maybe you've been there, too, where the pain is so intense that it feels like there's no way out.

But here's what I've learned: when we turn to God, even in our most broken state, He hears us. He doesn't just listen—He actively moves to deliver us from the fears that paralyze us. It doesn't always mean that the circumstances immediately change, but He changes us in the middle of them. He gives us the strength to face another day, the courage to take another step, and the assurance that we are not alone.

Surviving trauma is a process, and it's okay to acknowledge that it's hard. But in seeking the Lord, there is a deliverance that goes beyond just surviving—it's about finding peace in the storm, hope in the despair, and knowing that God is with you every step of the way.

Questions:

1. Can you recall a time when fear seemed overwhelming, but you sought God and experienced His deliverance? How did that change your perspective or situation?

2. In what ways can you actively seek the Lord in the middle of your current fears or traumas?

3. How does knowing that God listens and delivers give you hope in healing from past traumatic events?

Prayer:

God, I am so grateful for everything You have healed in me. You are the Lord of my life and all I want to do is serve You. Thank You for Your deliverance, grace, love, and freedom. Thank You for exposing every fear and covering them with hope and Your Word. Bring people to mind who need to hear more about You. Open doors so wide to share about You that the only thing I can do is run through them. I pray for divine appointments. In Jesus's name, Amen.

"I sought the Lord, and He answered me and delivered me from all my fears."

PSALM 34:4
(ESV)

Chapter 13

Surviving the Darkest Valleys

by Christa Crookston

I spent the first few years after my divorce numbing my pain by saying I had "moved on." I didn't exactly know how to grieve the losses I had experienced and I was determined to find a new husband and start a new family as fast as I possibly could. I wanted to prove I was worthy, I was wanted, and that he had made a mistake. I wanted to prove I was over it and that I had moved on, acting as though I was perfectly fine.

I learned that pretending to be fine wasn't the same as actually being fine. There were times I thought I'd never survive. Sometimes I'd ask myself, "How did I end up here?" Thank goodness God is much wiser than me and much more patient. When I was ready, He was there and walked with me through some really tough times to bring me closer to Him, which led to real healing. Every step of the way, he provided His insight through great friends and mentors to help me along the way. In my renewed relationship with Christ, I found hope. Eventually, I discovered how to grieve, inventory my losses, and just sit. I learned how to stop wearing "Divorce" on my chest like a scarlet letter. I found just how much my God loved me despite the shame and guilt I felt. I wouldn't trade anything I have gone through because God has used every ounce of pain to make me into the person I am today.

My road to healing had more twists and turns, ups and downs, and detours than I ever expected when I started. I have learned that you've never really finished healing from trauma and tragedy, but you learn how to process the pockets of grief that pop up from time to time. My road to healing is special and unique to me, just as yours will be to you. I can't compare God's plan for me to His plan for you. What I can promise is when I humbled myself and sought God, I found him in a big way. I have such joy and peace in my life now, and with God's help and strength, you will, too.

Don't let tragedy define you. Use it to grow, become stronger, and bring you closer to God, but don't let it be who you are. For me, divorce became something I went through, like a root canal, an open heart surgery, or a tax audit, but it didn't define who I was or who I am. Who I am is a blessed and loved child of God.

Here are a few truths that I lived by that helped me during those times and that I still use today.

1) I remember Christ and his love for me. I learned that God doesn't hate or think less of me; He loves me. In Jeremiah 31:3 (NIV), the Lord said, "I have loved you with an everlasting love; I have drawn you with unfailing kindness." That is exactly how I felt—that God was drawing me closer with his unfailing kindness and love.

2) I gained a support system, a life coach, a gym family, and a church family. I attended a support group called Divorce Care, and I had my amazing family and my awesome newfound friends. I read many books on personal growth and leadership. I learned about different love languages

and personality types. I read books on marriage and divorce. Most importantly, I read God's word and His promises.

3) I did my best to keep a positive attitude. I kept scriptures and positive messages around me all the time. I began to lean on and trust God during the hard times. With my pride and ego out of the way, I was able to hear the hard things and truths that led me to positive change and growth.

One promise in Scripture I clung to was Jeremiah 29:11-13 in the Message version:

> "I'll show up and take care of you as I promised and bring you back home. I know what I am doing. I have it all planned out—plans to take care of you, not abandon you, plans to give you the future you hope for. When you call on me, when you come and pray to me, I'll listen. When you come looking for me, you'll find me...I'll turn things around for you...I'll bring you back from...exile. You can count on it."

In the years since, by God's grace, I have grown in so many ways. God has been faithful in His love for me. I'm here today to tell you there is a beautiful, wonderful life after tragedy. I'm here to tell you that you are beautiful, you are intelligent, and you are worth it. I promise God is with you in the darkness of the valley. He is faithful. His love endures, and He will never leave you or forsake you. Do not let your present circumstances cause you to forget the promises God has laid out for you in his Word.

Today, I'm happily married to an amazing man who is an equally amazing husband and father to our six children. I could not imagine when I was enduring that dark valley the blessings God had in store for me.

NOTE: On April 17, 2023, Christa's beloved husband, Dave, passed away in his sleep at the age of 51. His death rocked his family as he left behind six amazing children. During this time, she also found out and battled cancer for the fourth time. Christa still stands as the epitome of survival and trusting in God, even when she doesn't know how she will make it to the next second of the day. As her friend, getting to be an eyewitness to both the love they had for each other and the love they have for God was not only the most beautiful relationship I had seen, but also seeing the community come together to help her and her children inspired me to keep going as well.

Reflection with Gina:

In Christa's episode, she talks about the impact Jeremiah 29:11 has had in every area of her life. This verse can be difficult to handle sometimes. I recently attended calling hours for a friend's father, who was four years younger than me. I looked at my friend and my heart broke. I know she is having a difficult time seeing how this verse could be good and encouraging to her right now because she now has to live the rest of her life without her dad. She is not alone in this because I have felt this way, too. God is good and only does good, but what good can come from this instance or that instance? These are questions we may never understand on this side of heaven.

Here is what I do know. I have walked through grief, loss, and survival on so many different levels, yet there is one constant: God. Whether I knew it or not, God was always there. He was still working, planning, and guiding me toward something good. Sometimes, the healing doesn't come in the way we expect. It can be a process that takes longer than we'd like. But through it all, we can trust that God's hand is on our lives, shaping our future with hope.

In the middle of our pain, it can be hard to see God's plan. We might question why we are going through such difficult times. But Jeremiah 29:11 reminds us that even in the middle of our struggles, God is preparing us for something better. He's using our pain to grow us, deepen our faith, and bring us closer to Him. He will also use our pain to walk with others as they experience similar situations. Our healing journey is part of His plan, and it's a plan filled with hope.

Questions:

1. Reflect on a time when you faced a difficult season. How did you see God's hand in your healing process, even if it wasn't obvious at the time?

2. How can you trust in God's plan for your future, even when the path to healing feels slow or uncertain?

3. What steps can you take today to lean into the hope that God's plans for you are good despite any current challenges or pain?

Prayer:

God, the struggles I am going through are too much for me to handle. I lift my hands to You and in doing this, I give the struggles to You. Take control of my relationship that is in the pits and guide me into Your will to restore what can and should be restored. Help me to walk away if that is what needs to happen. Give me knowledge and insight to know the restoration that needs to happen is in my heart and mind. Show me your love and reveal to me the promises You have made in these verses. Help me to get connected to You. In Jesus's name, Amen.

"I'll show up and take care of you as I promised and bring you back home. I know what I am doing. I have it all planned out – plans to take care of you, not abandon you, plans to give you the future you hope for. When you call on me, when you come and pray to me, I'll listen. When you come looking for me, you'll find me.....I'll turn things around for you.....I'll bring you back from...exile. You can count on it."

JEREMIAH 29:11-13
(MSG)

Chapter 14

Surviving the Critics

By Kat Vazquez

With over 20 years in the media industry, I started my career in broadcasting as an on-air news reporter. Having worked for various television and radio news outlets, some of my assignments required me to be a "one-man band," where I learned the many facets of broadcast production in the field. I learned how to shoot, edit, produce, and on some occasions, even live-direct news shows. These experiences deepened my convictions as a journalist but also helped me learn how to push boundaries artistically in my storytelling. My passion for creativity in news stories garnered acclaim, landing me prestigious television journalism awards as well as getting many of my news stories picked up by the network news.

Though my career was fulfilling, I was beginning to feel as though there was more I was called to do. I began to pray for God's best in my life. Was there a family in my future? Was I meant to be involved in more than just reporting the news? Almost as if it was an answer-back, a strange and painful turn of events at work caused me to question my purposes, not only as a journalist but in my own voice. Before, I was known as an overachiever, but at that time, I felt like a shell of a person. I was depressed, doubting my own worth and believing the lying voices of the devil as if they were my own.

Unable to fake it on camera any longer, I resigned from the station and returned back to my hometown to seek healing. During my two-year restoration journey, the Lord began connecting all the dots. He was using my pain to remove me from a toxic situation the enemy meant for my destruction, but God took me down the path of meeting my future husband. In God's brilliant and grace-filled ways, He was answering my prayers. He was redirecting my life to bring about His best.

As the years rolled by, Jorge Vazquez and I were married, and God gave us two precious boys. However, I still struggled with a need to be productive for God and tried to earn His favor. I didn't feel that I was worthy of love or even to receive love. The residue was still festering from the lying patterns of my past.

I began journaling my feelings of unworthiness and addressing my need to feel validated by my performance. Had I ever stopped to receive and recognize my heavenly Father's perfect love and know who I really was as His daughter? I wrote down my questions and captured the scriptures He was speaking to me. He was showing me my real identity as His own daughter. I was a citizen of heaven living on earth, I was chosen before the creation of the world, and God had a special plan for my life filled with hope and a future. When I fully grasped the truth of being an heir of God and a sister to Christ Jesus, my mind was blown! Suddenly, I awakened to a truth older than time: I was thought of before my birth, creatively designed, filled with purpose, and created to give Him joy just by being in His family. It was a huge concept that was so beautiful, and it brought much healing to my wounded heart.

As the years followed, my journals filled while I grappled with and further understood revelation into this relational identity. I would press in, listening to the Lord's response during my quiet times. The responses were golden nuggets about our real identity and how we are to live as sons and daughters of God. We are the *Ecclesia*, a term in the Bible that means His activated church, the saints. Our purpose is to expand His kingdom here on earth. We are the emerging bride of Christ, called to rule and reign with Him. We are called to be world changers. We are called to be the influencers. When we partner with Father's heart and want what He wants, it is then that we can pull heaven's culture down to earth.

It is my greatest privilege to see people step into their God-given purposes and live fully alive in everything Calvary's cross afforded them. In light of that, I knew this truth had to be shared. After years of writing, I released a devotional book on who we rightfully are as His and what that means. *REIGN: Restoring Identity*[1] is a field guide on how to recognize, behave and walk in all that it means to be a son or daughter of God. Filled with ruthless and defiant faith, we are the emerging bride of Christ. We are called to reign along with Him, pulling heaven down to earth.

---

1. Vazquez, Kat. (2022) *Reign: Restoring Identity.* Lightning Publishers

Reflection with Gina:

> "But you are a chosen race, a royal priesthood, a holy nation, a people for his possession, so that you may proclaim the praises of the one who called you out of darkness into his marvelous light."
>
> —1 Peter 2:9 (CSB)

How many times have you wondered if you were doing the things God intended for you to do? I have questioned this multiple times in my life. I have dealt with this in my vocation and relationships and even within the church community. I believe it is a part of our experience to feel this way at times because it leads us down a path of greater personal discovery and a deeper understanding of God's plan for our lives.

I wanted to help with a ministry, yet I did not know how, when, or why. But when I did, I found myself in a situation where I was not confident in my abilities and didn't know if it was the right path for me. Little did I know that through a conversation, conference, and class, I would come to discover exactly what God was calling me to do. I wasn't supposed to help someone else's ministry; I was supposed to lead the one God had specifically laid out for me. Now, I am embarking on a journey I would never have imagined myself on, especially at the age of 45.

God has called each one of us for a specific purpose at this specific moment in time. Kat found out what God was calling her to do after she gave up her idea and followed Him for the next right step. What next step is God calling you to take? Start by asking Him and moving yourself out of the way and see what He does.

Questions:

1. What are areas in my life where I am feeling uneasy or feel a stirring that a change is coming?

2. What is stopping me from completely going after God's plan for my life?

3. Where are the places or areas where my God-given talents intersect with the next step God wants me to take?

Prayer:

God, I thank You for leading me. Thank you for helping me survive toxic situations that were meant to take me out. Help me seek Your plan for my life by taking an honest look at each area of my life, including going back to childhood. Help me rediscover the joy You have given me and draw on the strength You have given me to keep going every day. Open doors to where You want me placed and shut the doors to the places where I am not supposed to be. I trust Your leading. In Jesus's name, Amen.

"But you are a chosen race, a royal priesthood, a holy nation, a people for his possession, so that you may proclaim the praises of the one who called you out of darkness into his marvelous light"

1 PETER 2:9
(CSB)

Chapter 15

Surviving Addiction

By George A. Wood

I was born eight years after the last of my four older siblings. By the time I was in kindergarten, my father abandoned me. He divorced my mother, left her penniless with three kids in upstate New York, and ran off to Florida with a much younger woman. My eldest brother Mark left with him, and James left a year later. This left me with no healthy male influences in my life.

Roughly a year later, Mark died in a construction accident where my father was foreman, creating even deeper family resentment and division. My two sisters, Linda and Sue, left New York and joined my father and brother to try to rebuild the family down south, leaving my mom and I in the dust.

These traumatic events changed how my parents viewed life—and how they viewed me—forever. To them, I was an inconvenience at best, a physical representation of a family that would never be. My dad's hope faded quickly. After his son died and his girlfriend left, he fell into addiction. Mom did her best to pick up the pieces and make ends meet, but with nobody left except for me to lean on, she began to drink heavily.

My parents may have loved me in their own broken way, but they no longer had time or space to parent me.

My broken family situation fueled my broken identity. I felt lost and alone, and I was willing to do anything to feel loved. When I was 13 years old, my father's girlfriend crawled into my bed after a night of drinking and had sex with me. From that defining moment forward, I thought sex was love and alcohol was the best way to get there. So, like the confused kid I was, I went after it all. I began drinking and engaging in sexual activity with my peers. Women became objects, something to conquer and dispose of. Real relationships became foreign, which multiplied my pain and confusion. I balanced middle and high school sports with as much sex and alcohol as I could possibly get. Sports-related injuries led to three major surgeries; those surgeries led to unmonitored painkillers. That careless mix of alcohol, sex, and opioids kept me so numb that I still can't remember most of the nineties.

After the blur that was college, I graduated with my bachelor's degree and moved back to Tampa, where I partied with my father as well as my brother James and my sister Sue on weekends. We sunk deeper and deeper into denial about our struggles.

On the surface, I looked like I had it all. I found a great job and built a successful career. I found a nice girl and married her, and we had a beautiful son, River. I was deeply addicted but highly functional, or so I thought. In 2002, I had a nervous breakdown—one so severe I crawled inside a bottle of vodka for six months. My budding marriage, family, career, and life were dissolving right in front of me, and I felt powerless to do anything about it. My wife rightfully divorced me, taking my one-year-old son with her. I lost everything, including my will to live.

In the years that followed, my addiction, mental health problems, and suicidal thoughts owned me. I made genuine attempts at recovery, walking through 12-step programs, rehabs, and counseling, many of them faith-based. I bulldozed my way through a trail of detox units and psychiatric wards, on suicide watch wherever I went. My ex-wife, newly remarried, made her best attempt to honor supervised visitation with River—even though I was behind on child support. She showed me more grace than I deserved. But her confidence in me waned as I experienced relapse time and again. When a failed suicide attempt got me kicked out of rehab, she asked me to give up all parental rights and give our son a chance at a better life. I adamantly refused, but deep down, I knew she was right. He would be better off without an addict for a father. I was coldly escorted out of the rehab facility without a clue what to do or where to go. So, I tried something desperate—something I'd never tried before. Scuffling down the street with my entire life in a duffel bag, I cried out to heaven in desperation.

"God, either kill me or do something. I know this isn't funny to you."

Now, I always believed in God, but I also believed I was hell-bound. It's what my parents told me. It's what the world told me. It's what the church told me. I knew God existed, but I thought He was angry with me, so I steered clear. Because I couldn't wrap my head around earthly relationships, I didn't yet understand that God loved me in a way no earthly father ever could.

God met me in that last-ditch cry for help with a phone call. It was Luke, a Christian friend I'd met in a recovery house a few months earlier. "Hey man, are you okay?" he asked. "God told me to drop everything and call you right away because you needed help." God had never been more real to me. For the first time in my life, I wanted to know more about who he really was. Luke took me in and introduced me to "Pops," one of his spiritual mentors. Pops introduced me to the real Jesus—the real way to the real Father.

So, I got saved and I got sober.

Then I relapsed.

I got saved again and sober again.

Then I relapsed again.

The vicious cycle continued as the words of all those well-meaning pastors, counselors, and recovery leaders over the years echoed in my mind.

Just come to Jesus and you'll be okay.

Just come to Jesus and you'll be set free.

Just come to Jesus and you'll never use again.

Truth be told, I was about ready to have a come-to-Jesus moment with every single person who had spewed these quick-fix, phony platitudes at me. Sure, I'd heard miraculous stories of alter calls and healing prayers that broke off addiction, mental health problems, and suicidal thoughts instantaneously and for good. It was inspiring, but it wasn't my reality. Where was my miracle? Why was I relapsing? How could I get saved and sober, again and again, and still struggle? I started to doubt whether the kind of transformed life God was offering was really for someone like me.

Whenever a relapse happened, Pops always saw it coming. He always gave me the freedom to choose, and when I chose poorly, he was always there waiting to welcome me home and restore me gently. But in 2006, after a particularly tough go-around with the bottle, Pops laid it all on the line, not with an ultimatum, but with a high-challenge, spirit-led spiritual shaking. "That's enough," he said. "It's time you realize God's grace has brought you this far."

That relapse was my last relapse. Pops became the loving earthly father I always needed, and God revealed himself as the loving Heavenly Father I never knew he was. For the first time, I stepped into the transformed life he had waiting for me—a promised-land life that was worth staying sober for.

In 2007, I stepped into ministry as a recovery leader in Orlando and helped build a men's addiction program called Vision of God Ministries. When one of the other leaders relapsed, I was quickly promoted to the position of pastor and went all-in with my call. I had a passion and a purpose for the first time ever. I helped broken men get free, I developed real-world construction skills, and I was able to provide at least some child support to my ex-wife for River.

I stayed until the provision ran out—too long, in retrospect. I felt God leading me back to Tampa. But I had no plan. I had no money. I'd be crashing on Pops' couch. So, I had no choice but to lean completely on God to make a way for what he had called me to do.

Through a supernaturally timed series of encounters in a single weekend, God began to pull his plan together through his people. I met Carlos, one of my spiritual fathers, and his daughter Carla, who prophesied over me and invited me back into my true identity. I met Jason and his wife Katy, who became my best friends and ministry champions. I met future benefactors, who hired me to provide live-in care and recovery services for their addicted son in a million-dollar beach house on the Gulf of Mexico that was just five minutes away from where River lived. I couldn't have asked for or imagined a more perfect situation.

Once again, I was helping broken men get free. Once again, I was developing real-world skills and real-kingdom connections. I was not only able to provide some child support for River; I was able to repay the full amount of child support that my ex-wife had deferred and forgiven me—every single dime. She was overwhelmed by my transformation and moved with compassion to reunite me with my three-year-old son at the beach house. I'm forever grateful for her reckless grace to me. River, who is now at Gustavus Adolphus College on a football scholarship, says his first memories of me are in that peace-filled place. God did it all—and his grace was more than sufficient, even for me.

So many men in addiction say they want to be good fathers. When you trust God and let him Father you, it creates a ripple effect that can change a family tree for good. From that place of restoration and reconciliation, the momentum grew. I started helping the most desperate men I could find—many of them homeless heroin addicts who had been despised and rejected by traditional recovery programming. I was hired by an organization called The Underground to remodel old furniture into office space, and they encouraged me to hire the men I was loving and leading through recovery to help with the labor. I was able to offer them income, connections, and a renewed sense of purpose while working with and ministering to them daily—much like the apostle Paul and his protégé Timothy did. Even then, the Lord was equipping me to go deeper.

In late 2009, I began laying the groundwork for The Timothy Initiative, widely known as "T.I.," a community designed to house and empower men in recovery from addiction for as long as it takes to build a life that is worth staying sober. The ministry launched publicly in 2010 and continues to thrive.

Then along came Julie—my wife, my partner, and my equal in everything. I never dreamed I would be blessed with a second chance to be a God-honoring husband. But let me tell you—God is in the business of restoration. I'm convinced the day he made me, he knew I would need her.

Every time I see her and watch the desires of our hearts come to life through the work of our hands, I think, "Okay, God, now you're just showing off." When I married this smart, passionate, beautiful powerhouse for the kingdom in 2011, we became a family on mission. She felt God calling her to a separate but parallel ministry path called The Just Initiative, which launched in 2016 as an organization committed to building community across typical economic and racial divides to create pathways out of systemic poverty for women and children at risk of homelessness. Little did we know, God's collective call wouldn't stop there. In 2020, I birthed a third ministry, The Sober Truth Project. Our goal is to show the world the value of vulnerability over anonymity and total life transformation over baseline sobriety through education, advocacy and practical support to help the world see recovery and the role faith plays in recovery differently.

Today, each of these ministries offers unapologetically Christ-centered, Holy Spirit-led transformation and hope for a promised land life. Our goal is to change the way the world sees recovery so that people who are struggling with addiction, mental health problems, and suicidal thoughts aren't forced to do recovery in the margins. Recovery isn't just our ministry; it's our life. Julie and I actually live and work in the communities we've built together. We do every part of life with the people we've been called to love and lead through recovery. We own and steward multiple homes in underserved, crime-ridden, poverty-stricken, inner-city Tampa, where we all live together as family. We minister to the surrounding area by counseling, supporting, and advocating for hundreds more men and women who are actively building promised land lives that are worth staying sober for. We are committed to living out an unconventional following of Jesus in a radical community lifestyle. Every precious life we see transformed by God's grace provides consistent affirmation that Julie and I are exactly where we're meant to be.

Reflection with Gina:

> "I have been crucified with Christ, and I no longer live, but Christ lives in me. The life I now live in the body, I live by faith in the Son of God, who loved me and gave himself for me."
>
> —Galatians 2:20 (CSB)

This verse is the definition of our Christian walk. It is also not the easiest process because it must take place on a daily basis. It's not for our salvation because that is fully accomplished through Jesus's death, burial and resurrection. But it is the giving over of our lives and the repentance over how we fail. God is not standing over us with a red marker, ready to scratch us out of heaven when we mess up. That is why the blood of Jesus was shed, which is the only red mark we need.

Just like George, I tried to get "re-saved" more times than I can count. I became a Christian in the late 1990s during the purity movement, and that was an area in which I really struggled. Every time a thought entered my mind or I acted on an impulse, I would recite the sinner's prayer to "save my soul" again. Instead of repenting and leaning on the grace and salvation I already had through Jesus, I thought I needed more. This was until God opened my eyes and put someone in my path, just like George, who set me straight. That person helped me understand God loved me despite my shortcomings because He already knew them and still sent Jesus to die for me.

What situation(s) in your life can you look back on and see how the hand of God was there, carrying you through and leading you away from the people and places that would destroy you? Take some time today to journal through them and reflect on just how much God has helped you. As you journal, consider how these experiences have shaped your faith and strengthened your reliance on God's grace.

Questions:

1. Can you identify a time in your life when you struggled with the concept of grace and felt the need to "earn" your salvation repeatedly? Reflect on how understanding God's unchanging love and grace has transformed your relationship with Him.

2. How can you daily live out Galatians 2:20, embracing the truth that Christ lives in you? Think about practical steps you can take to surrender your life to Him and walk in the freedom of His grace.

Prayer:

God, I thank You that as I reflect on all of the situations in my life that were meant to take me out, I can see Your hands moving. I can look back and see what You have done and what You have brought me out of and where I am standing now. If I am still stuck in the muck of my own mess, I am reaching out to You to help me like You did for George and Gina. Guide me to the people who will lead me closer to You. Lead me to the beginning of my new life in and with You. In Jesus's name, Amen.

"I have been crucified with Christ, and I no longer live, but Christ lives in me. The life I now live in the body, I live by faith in the Son of God, who loved me and gave himself for me"

GALATIANS 2:20
(CSB)

Chapter 16

Surviving the False Narratives

by Lindsay Griswold

One of my biggest regrets was not knowing my Bible and being deceived by a false religion. I grew up Christian. I didn't read my Bible habitually, but I was involved in youth group and went to church. I had a relationship with God in high school, and I constantly talked to him throughout my day. But I didn't deeply know him because I wasn't steeped in His Word.

I was introduced to the Church of Jesus Christ of Latter-Day Saints (also known as LDS or Mormon) right after high school. I was told, "It's just like Christianity! We consider ourselves Christian." I heard that over and over throughout the next several years. Honestly, I didn't really know what Christianity was or fully understand what I believed because I had never spent time in my Bible. LDS Missionaries came to my house to teach me lessons, and it did seem like Christianity. At the time, the main difference I was taught was baptism. Baptism in Mormonism is equal to salvation. You are forgiven for your sins through not just repentance but also baptism. The other difference was they claimed they had the true gospel. An angel spoke to their prophet and gave them another gospel, as well as much more to the scriptures, such as temples and baptisms for the dead.

Still, because I didn't know the Bible, it sounded good to me. I was baptized as LDS. I became involved in every aspect of the church. I went to the temple for the ceremonies; I had a "calling" (what LDS refers to as serving in the church) in the children's nursery. I spent three hours every Sunday at church. I went to all the church events. I invited other women to come to my house every month to teach me (they are referred to as "visiting teachers"). Eventually, I became a visiting teacher for other women, too.

But I didn't quite fit in. The first time I really noticed it was when I was asked to pray at a church meeting. I finished my prayer, and many women said, "She prays like a convert!" I didn't know there was a specific way to pray, but I quickly learned, after listening to others pray, that their prayers did sound so similar. It always started with "Lord, Heavenly Father" - never God, or just Lord. Usually, you should add that you are grateful for the church. Joseph Smith's name is usually thrown in there as well. I also didn't fit in because I had a tattoo, which I was asked to have removed. I didn't know all the church terms, but I threw myself into the church. I gave up coffee since it is not allowed. I wore a long skirt, learned to speak as a Mormon does, and attempted to be the best Mormon I could be.

Everything changed after I had my first child. I got postpartum depression and I began to question my faith. Not my faith in God but in the church. I felt like I was constantly striving. The Mormon culture was exhausting. Works to Mormonism are necessary for salvation. They believe they are saved by grace after they do all they can do (go to the temple, follow the word of wisdom, serve in the church, etc). They believe God will bless them with eternal life if they do their part. I felt like no matter how often I went to the temple or how much I served, I wasn't doing enough. On top of that, I found out things about that church that were kept hidden from me when I first joined.

One day, I was struggling emotionally. While scrolling through social media, a mini devotional popped up. It was from a Christian ministry and I remember instantly feeling like this was what was missing in my life. It was a deep love for God's Word, not a bunch of rules. It reminded me that I didn't have a relationship with God anymore. I was so busy trying to do things the "right" way that I had stopped praying to God. I ran and grabbed my Bible. It was an old Bible my dad had given me, not a Mormon version, and I opened it up to Genesis and started reading. My goal was to get back to basics with God. I decided to read His Word, stop striving so much, and have a relationship with Him again. I quit my calling at church. I was asked to speak at church, and I declined. I was told that no one declined, but I did.

I asked other Mormons if they had doubts, or I would bring up some inconsistencies the Book of Mormon had, but I was always told to ask the Holy Spirit and he would tell me the church was true. It took me about a year, but I read through the whole Bible. The moment I finished, I knew the LDS church wasn't true. I cried because I was deceived, but I found a relationship with God again. Getting out of a false religion can be hard because the theology is different. Upon becoming a Christian again, I read through the entire Bible another time so I could know for myself what I believed. Since the day I left the LDS church, I have been in God's Word every day. His Word is life to me. I know I don't have to strive with works for God. I wish I had the discernment before to recognize what is true and what is false, but God taught me a lot during that time. I am grateful God didn't leave me in that situation but offered me true freedom with Him.

Reflection with Gina:

> "Finally, be strengthened by the Lord and by his vast strength. Put on the full armor of God so that you can stand against the schemes of the devil. For our struggle is not against flesh and blood, but against the rulers, against the authorities, against the cosmic powers of this darkness, against evil, spiritual forces in the heavens. For this reason take up the full armor of God, so that you may be able to resist in the evil day, and having prepared everything, to take your stand. Stand, therefore, with truth like a belt around your waist, righteousness like armor on your chest, and your feet sandaled with readiness for the gospel of peace. In every situation take up the shield of faith with which you can extinguish all the flaming arrows of the evil one. Take the helmet of salvation and the sword of the Spirit — which is the word of God. Pray at all times in the Spirit with every prayer and request, and stay alert with all perseverance and intercession for all the saints."
>
> —Ephesians 6:10–18 (CSB)

I became a Christian when I was 16 and my parents bought me a Precious Moments statue called "Onward Christian Soldier." I still have it to this day. I have studied these verses in numerous different Bible studies and part of my ministry name came out of these verses. Still, I find it difficult to use them to fight my battles.

Ephesians 6:10–18 is a powerful reminder that our Christian walk is a battleground, not a playground. We are engaged in a spiritual war, and the enemy is relentless. But God, in His infinite wisdom and grace, has not left us defenseless. He has provided us with the full armor of God to stand firm against the schemes of the devil. The imagery of armor is not just poetic; it's practical. The belt of truth keeps us grounded in the reality of God's Word so we are not swayed by the lies of the enemy. The breastplate of righteousness guards our hearts, reminding us that our righteousness comes from Christ alone, not our own efforts. Our feet are sandaled with the readiness of the gospel of peace, allowing us to walk confidently in our calling, even in the face of chaos. The shield of faith protects us from the flaming arrows of doubt, fear, and temptation, while the helmet of salvation assures us of our secure identity in Christ.

Then there's the sword of the Spirit, which is the Word of God. This is our only offensive weapon, but it's more than enough. With it, we can cut through the enemy's lies and stand firm in the truth. But we don't wield this weapon alone; we must be in constant prayer, staying alert and persevering in intercession for ourselves and others.

The Christian life isn't easy, but we're not fighting this battle on our own. God has given us everything we need to stand firm. The question is, are we putting on the full armor of God daily, or are we going into battle unprepared?

Questions:

1. Which piece of the armor of God do you find yourself needing the most in this season of your life? How can you intentionally put it on each day?

2. Reflect on a time when you felt spiritually attacked. How did you respond? How can you better equip yourself with the armor of God for future battles?

3. Prayer is a crucial part of spiritual warfare. How can you deepen your prayer life to stay alert and persevere in the face of the enemy's attacks?

Prayer:

God, thank You for leaving us with Your armor to use against the tactics of the enemy. I repent because this is not the first place I go when the attacks come. Help me to remember to pray this every day before my feet hit the ground and my hand goes to my phone. This armor is the physical representation of what is happening spiritually, and I need it at all times. I want to be a soldier in Your army and I know it starts here. The more prepared I am ahead of time, the more it becomes second nature. Remind me just as you did for Lindsay to seek You in Your Word to stand my ground. In Jesus's name, Amen.

"Finally, be strengthened by the Lord and by his vast strength. Put on the full armor of God so that you can stand against the schemes of the devil...Pray at all times in the Spirit with every prayer and request, and stay alert with all perseverance and intercession for all the saints."

EPHESIANS 6:10-11 & 18
(CSB)

Chapter 17

Healing From Body Shame

by Heather Creekmore

I guess you could call me a visionary. I knew exactly where I wanted to go and how to get there. *Or, so I thought.*

I cut her picture out of the magazine and put it on the inside of a journal. Sure, some preferred to place these cutouts on the fridge door or by their mirror, but I didn't want my goals to be that overt. The inside cover of my little book of secret thoughts would get the job done.

She was probably five foot ten, which I conveniently ignored because there was nothing I could do to affect my height. But, I was certain, with the right amount of determination and willpower, I could get her figure. Less ice cream. Extra trips around the track. Morning push-ups. I'd look at my calendar to decide the date by which this magical transformation needed to occur—major holidays, vacations, or birthdays worked fine. Any event that included photo ops offered an incentivized deadline.

Her hair. That would require another trick to accomplish. Try a few more styling products. Let it grow out. Find a "better" hairdresser. Surely, it couldn't be that hard to glow up my locks. *A girl has to have goals, right?*

These were mine. *Look better. Be better. Morph, mold, shape and form myself into someone who would make me proud.* Become that woman who makes everyone take a second glance. I believed this type of transformation was the only way to cure my body shame. If I could just look like *that* woman, if I could become her — surely my struggles would melt away.

It started around third grade. I looked in the full-length mirror of my bedroom and decided my thighs were too big. As I glanced around during gym class, I decided my legs were bigger. By middle school, I was dieting with my mom. By high school, I decided dieting wasn't enough, and I would see how long I could go without eating. Back in the 1990s, we didn't know to call this an eating disorder, but I'm certain it was. I lost my period for most of my sophomore year of college. I was never underweight and no one knew how I struggled not to think about food and calories all day long. Now I see the mental anguish and physical toll my starve and binge cycle took on all aspects of my health.

I dabbled in exercise, finding it an efficient and effective way to keep my body slim while still eating all the brownies I wanted. I even became a fitness instructor because I was certain those women leading aerobics classes loved their bodies. Of course, it only took leading one kickboxing class to send that myth the way of Santa Claus and the Easter Bunny. I soon learned that even the women who worked at the gym struggled with their body image.

Striving, starving, and trying everything to shrink myself permeated my life. I called myself a Christian. I knew the scriptures. But somehow, reading that God looked at the heart or that I had been "fearfully and wonderfully made" was never enough. Deep down, I wondered if God had cheated me. Perhaps others were born with "wonderfully made" bodies, but it was up to me to take what God had made and improve it.

That woman inside my journal haunted me. Her image promised to give me everything I ever desired. If I could just look like her, I'd have freedom and joy I'd never experienced. If I could just be like her—disciplined, organized, determined—then I'd unlock the key to eternal happiness. I could just taste it.

Her image had stealthily become my real god. Sure, I said I wanted to be like Jesus. Yet I spent a lot more of my time and money trying to become more like her. *Her gorgeous cut arms, her thigh gap, her thin waist, narrow nose, and brilliant hair... loving her was easy.* Loving that image made me hate myself all the more. She reinforced every lie the enemy was screaming in my head like *you aren't good enough, you aren't valuable, if you could lose weight or change your body, then life would be better.* She shamed and condemned me for every cookie or missed workout. Loving Jesus seemed disconnected from my real mission of becoming more beautiful.

Eventually, God showed me how her image had become an idol. Like King Josiah, I had to tear down this idol and rip that photo out of my journal and my heart. I confessed how I'd longed to be more like an image than like my savior. I'd fixed my eyes on my thighs instead of on Him.

Now, I've had the opportunity to walk with hundreds of women who have faced similar battles. Some have endured full-blown eating disorders; others have faced a lifelong battle with the scale or the mirror—believing the same lie I did. It sounds like, "As soon as I get the body I want, then I'll be free." I see now how this is just a lie. Supermodels struggle with body image issues. The only path to freedom is not through changing your appearance, but by changing where you find your acceptance. We can spend our whole lives on a quest to try to love our bodies, but what God really asks of us (and the secret to true freedom) is to love Him and love others.

When we discover that all that we need and long for is found in him, it changes the importance of our quest to look like anyone else. We are then freed not to love our bodies, but to love Him and understand that our bodies, though important for carrying out his plan for our lives, were never created to be worshipped.

Reflection with Gina:

> "Now all glory to God, who is able, through his mighty power at work within us, to accomplish infinitely more than we might ask or think."
>
> —Ephesians 3:20 (NLT)

This chapter is incredibly important for me to include in this book. How many of us have dealt with body image issues? I'll be the first to raise my hands—and feet! This has been a struggle for me for as long as I can remember. I was the girl with big hair and huge lenses in her glasses. From the time I was five until I was thirteen, I was a ballet dancer in a small Christian dance company that focused on celebrating the beautiful creation we were made to be. There was no pressure to look a certain way, and I was free to be myself.

But when I was thirteen, everything changed. I still remember how the words of two boys affected me. One looked at my leg and asked why the front of it was so large—it was just my muscle, but his words hurt all the same. The other told me I needed to shave my legs and that I shouldn't be a dancer because it was stupid.

From then on, I started comparing myself to the women in magazines, movies, television shows, and even the other girls around me. Just like Heather, I had a specific image in my head of what true happiness would look like. As time went on, I noticed how differently I was treated based on my size and appearance. My worth felt tied to how I looked, and I've been on a roller coaster with my weight ever since. I'm not saying I still don't have moments where I look at pictures and think, "Ugh, bad angle," or "I look terrible." But overall, I've learned that my worth is not in my appearance but in who God made me to be. God looks at the heart (1 Samuel 16:7). The Creator of the world thought the world was incomplete without me. He knew my story and journey would help many other people, including you, who are holding this book right now.

When we fully open our lives to Him, He will do more than we could ever imagine, just as Ephesians 3:20 says. If we're still breathing, He's still working. He's not done with me, and He's not done with you.

Questions:

1. Consider Ephesians 3:20. Where in your life do you see God doing more than you could ever ask or imagine, even in areas where you are struggling? How can you open yourself up more fully to His continued work?

2. Think about the influence of society's standards on your self-image. How have you seen God reshape your understanding of true beauty and worth? What steps can you take to remind yourself daily that your value is rooted in who God says you are?

Prayer:

God, I thank You for creating me, even in all of my imperfections. I no longer want to be a slave to this yo-yo ride of trying to be what everyone else says I should be. I don't want to keep judging myself based on my appearance because in Your Word it says You look at my heart. Free me from the burden of self-image and self-esteem and lead me to more God-esteem and confidence in who You made me to be. In Jesus's name, Amen.

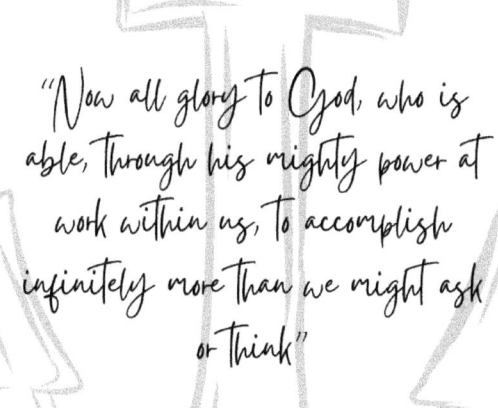

"Now all glory to God, who is able, through his mighty power at work within us, to accomplish infinitely more than we might ask or think"

EPHESIANS 3:20
(NLT)

SECTION 4

Healing

When most people think of the word "healing," they tend to think in physical terms. In the Bible, Jesus healed many people of physical afflictions, including diseases, blindness, deafness, even death itself. Jesus even addressed the mental side of healing when he asked the man by the pool of Bethesda who had been lying there for 38 years, "Would you like to get well?" (John 5:6 NLT). Jesus knew that healing actually begins in the mind and through the posture of our heart. In this section, there are stories of physical healing, as well as emotional, mental, and even relational healing. I pray that as you read each story, you are hearing the words of Jesus in your mind and heart and really consider what is stopping you from being truly freed and healed.

Chapter 18

Jesus Is the Answer

By Micah Lynn Hanson

I was born with an eye condition called amblyopia. Amblyopia is a condition where the vision in one of the eyes—the right eye, in my case—is reduced because the eye and the brain are not working together correctly. Although the eye itself looks normal, it is not being used to its ability and becomes increasingly weak since the brain is favoring the stronger eye. Normally, this is caught in infants, and it is easily corrected by simply patching the other eye—the strong eye—so that the brain is forced to use and strengthen the weaker eye that has not been getting used.

We didn't catch this condition until I was around six years old. At that time, my vision was 20/800. Since 800 is as far as the charts go, we don't really know how far off the charts my vision truly was. Suffice it to say, I was pretty dang blind.

The first doctor we went to said that there was nothing that he could do. He said that I was too "old" because my brain was too developed to start recognizing and using my weaker right eye. We were told that I would never be able to drive a car and that it would never even really be possible for me to wear glasses; the one lens would be so thick that the glasses would be off-balance and just fall off my face. This doctor told us that I would be recognized as handicapped for the rest of my life due to such poor vision.

There was an eye doctor in a neighboring town who specialized in this specific eye condition, but he was completely booked for months. My poor parents felt so helpless. Just days later, we found out that there was a last-minute cancellation, and I was able to get in with him the following week. After an entire day of dark rooms, blinding lights, and more eye drops than I could count, I was left blurry-eyed and unable to keep my eyes open even when the dimmest of lights was present. At the conclusion of this poking and prodding, the doctor sat my parents down and told us that he didn't have great news. There really was not much he could do. There are no surgeries for this condition, and the only form of therapy we could even try was the eye patching method commonly used on infants. He confirmed what the first doctor had told us about my brain being too developed for this method to really work and said, "Aside from a miracle, she'll never have the use of that eye."

Well, it just so happened that my family believed in the God of miracles. Our family and our entire church family started praying for healing in my eye. I started the eye patching process the next day.

That time in my little six-year-old self's life was difficult, to say the least. Not only was I basically completely blind for the first year or so of this therapy. When you wear a large adhesive bandage as a patch for 12+ hours a day, it becomes incredibly itchy and I was often left with horrible rashes all around my eye. Aside from the physical discomfort, it had also never really been a dream of mine to be a "one-eyed pirate" and have kids point and stare at me everywhere I went. Thinking back on it, I guess the upside to basically being blind was that I wasn't actually able to take note of the majority of the unwanted attention that I was getting.

I can still remember the very first day without the use of my good eye. I could not see even an inch in front of my face, so that day was filled with running into large inanimate objects, tripping over rocks in our garden, and even flipping right out of a hammock. Needless to say, I was miserable. I couldn't play outside without harming myself, I couldn't read, and I couldn't even see a television to help the time pass. I was a gloomy, pathetic little girl, and all I wanted to do was sit on my mommy's lap and cry. My mother would sit with me, pray, and tell me just how much she wished she could carry my burden. She reminded me that only God could carry my heavy burden and that she knew He would do just that if I would just ask Him. The second day was not much different from the first. I was blind, itchy, and miserable, walking around feeling terribly sorry for my little self.

On the third morning, I remember waking up absolutely dreading having to put that awful patch on yet again and having to endure another sightless day. I didn't want to do it; I couldn't do it. I decided there was only one thing I could try. I took a deep breath and told Jesus that I just couldn't do this, that it was too hard, and I asked Him to carry my burden. This was my first prayer of faith! As a six-year-old girl, I got to experience His touch firsthand, and the change left a lifetime impact. My circumstances didn't change because I still had to wear the patch for the next three years. But I had an experience with my Savior, and I was never the same.

Jesus was "The Answer," and He still is!

Anytime I have to go through something difficult, anytime I am in pain and questioning God's plan, anytime doubt creeps in, I can look back on that experience. When I have questioned if God is real, and I have questioned that more than a few times, I would remember that half-blind, six-year-old me and how Jesus had touched me and answered my prayer on that third morning.

After three years of patching my good eye and with the aid of corrective lenses over the years, my vision is now 20/30. I never could have imagined how invaluable this experience would truly be for my life.

Unexpected Battle

I was hospitalized late one night after passing out on the kitchen floor due to blood loss from internal bleeding. I knew something was really off. The doctors didn't seem to think it was anything serious; they said not to worry, and I was sent home. One week later, I became so sick that I was bedridden for days on end while working outside the country. I was feverish, unable to eat, and losing an alarming amount of weight. I had to be flown back to the United States early so I could be seen by a doctor as quickly as possible.

After a series of tests and procedures, I was told I had Crohn's disease, and at that time, there was no known cure for this condition. There's really no way to describe that feeling when you are told that you have an incurable disease. I just sat there. It just didn't feel possible. I was completely unable to truly wrap my head around it for several months. I was a hard-working country girl who never got sick, I rarely ate fast food, and I exercised regularly...how could I have an incurable disease? In the months to follow, I remember often thinking, "Okay, the joke is over now; this isn't funny anymore! I can be healthy again!" Then, I had moments when I would just completely break down sobbing when I realized that this wasn't a joke or a bad dream and that I may indeed have to learn to live with this disease for the rest of my life. While this disease is still present in my body, and some days are better than others, I have been medication-free for well over a year now, and Crohn's disease no longer dictates my daily life.

I learned so much about God and his love for me and how he loved me so well through others during that time. I have had the sweetest, most amazing, and supportive people surrounding me and covering me with prayer through it all. While I wouldn't wish this disease on anyone, I am truly thankful for it in my life. I'm so beyond grateful for what it has taught me and how it has brought me closer to Jesus and made me a better, stronger, and more grateful person.

Rediscovering His Version of Me

Coming to the realization that I have allowed the entirety of my self-worth to be wrapped up in other people and what they think of me was an extremely humbling thing. The process it took to come to that realization included having people, my identity, and everything safe torn away from me. It felt excruciating, to say the least.

I wish that I could say that being incredibly insecure, never understanding my self-worth or my worth in Christ, was something that I just outgrew, but it all has too easily translated into my adulthood. It began manifesting itself in unhealthy and destructive relationships, living compulsively to please others out of fear, and many other forms of self-inflicted pain over the years. Thankfully, Jesus wasn't going to let me stay there. Due to my little world being completely shattered by some very painful personal experiences, I have been forced to face myself and all of my broken places. That's when God showed up.

Journeying from a place of self-loathing to a place of self-love, compassion, and acceptance has been anything but pleasant. But I am learning if we allow pain and discomfort to stretch us, God will use it to lead us into a better place. It is a place of health and balance where we never would have arrived if not for that specific pain. Through several months of intense soul searching, the gentle guidance of an amazing therapist and the unfailing love of our Lord, I am a completely changed person from who I was. I am a healed, more balanced individual, and I no longer have to live out of my fear and core wounds.

He was "The Answer" for a blind six-year-old. He has been "The Answer" through all of the tough days when my body turned against itself, and He will continue to be "The Answer" as I go forward, living my life to the absolute fullest!

Reflection with Gina:

> "Give all your worries and cares to God, for he cares about you."
>
> —1 Peter 5:7 (NLT)

In chapter 5 of 1 Peter, Peter begins by giving advice to the elders and young people in the church. He talks about how they should treat each other and exercise their responsibility for leading others. This is not an easy task for anyone, whether back then or today. When we lead others, either individually or collectively, we will be held accountable for how we did.

That is why Peter continues in the chapter by reminding us to give our cares and worries to God. Then, the next verse begins by warning everyone:

> "Stay alert! Watch out for your great enemy, the devil. He prowls around like a roaring lion, looking for someone to devour. Stand firm against him and be strong in your faith. Remember that your family of believers all over the world is going through the same kind of suffering you are."
>
> —1 Peter 5:8–9

This is a great reminder that no matter what challenge we face, we should first give it to God and then be ready to fight. We need to fight for our family, health, friends, church and anyone or anything else in our lives that the enemy would love to take out. This is why it is important to be in the

Word daily, speak it over every area of your life, and train others how to do the same.

Micah talks about how her own body was failing her at two different times and locations. She talked about how difficult it was to not see right and also how Crohn's disease ran her life. She chose to give her concerns and worries over to God, and now she gives us hope by reminding us Jesus is the answer to everything!

Questions:

1. What areas of your life are you holding onto with such a tight grip that a crowbar wouldn't be able to get it out of your hands?

2. Why are you holding onto it so tight? Are you afraid of losing control?

3. What would happen if you handed everything over to God today?

Prayer:

God, I confess that I have held onto my worries, cares and fears like a security blanket for a long time. I am so tired of carrying my burden and trying to handle it in my own strength. I release my tight grip and I give everything over to You. Take my burden from me and lead me to the place where I trust completely in You. I know You sent Your Son to cover everything in my life, beginning with my deepest concerns and struggles. I know You will give me the strength to care for those around me. Help me stand firm against the enemy's schemes and not give him a foothold. In Jesus's name, Amen.

Chapter 19

Healing From Fear

By Elle Cardel

As a child, I prayed the exact same prayer every single night. It went a little something like, *"As I lay me down to sleep, I pray the Lord my soul to keep. if I die before I wake, I pray the Lord my soul would take."* Perhaps you know it. I would wrap up this prayer by asking the Lord to bless my family and those who were homeless and to help me sleep well. I prayed this prayer for *years* because it was what I was taught. It was the only prayer I knew, and, more than anything, it was the final box to check at the end of the day in order to ensure God was "pleased" with me. This is how the story begins of swimming and nearly drowning in the dangerous waters of legalistic theology.

I was raised in the church, but I did not intimately know my Father in heaven until my late teen years. My entire childhood was spent fearing God in all the wrong ways. This was the unfortunate aftermath of being taught that His acceptance of me was based on law-keeping and performance. It looked a whole lot like obsessing over every little thing I could in order to properly measure up in God's eyes. I thought being driven by the fear of what God would do to me if I messed up was normal or even necessary.

The only love with which I was familiar was one not driven by grace but works.

As a child, this looked like hyper-fixating on being the "perfect" daughter and student. I strived for the best southern manners around and straight A's on every report card. I sought to excel in every extracurricular opportunity in which I participated, and I prided myself in being a people-pleaser any chance I could. My kind and generous acts weren't as selfless as they may have appeared. My life was driven by a constant hunger to be "good." In my mind, the more I did, the less sin-filled I was and the more God loved me.

As you can imagine, when I made mistakes, it felt like the end of the road, like I had been disqualified. I would convince myself it was too late and I was too far gone. I couldn't even bring my mistakes to God because all I could picture was disappointment. In my mind, I was no longer worth it. I would run from God until I couldn't run anymore. At that point, I would slowly turn around and drag myself back to His feet in utter desperation, apologizing and begging for yet another second chance. This was no way to live. Yet, I believed it was the only way to live.

The freeing revelation of God's unending mercy and grace had not yet washed over me. The legalistic shackles still had their grip on me. I longed for –I *needed*–God to love me. Little did I know, however, that the only perfect thing in my life was, indeed, God's love for me. It was there from the very beginning, and it would be there, ready to greet me with its warm embrace once the scales were removed from my eyes.

I'll never forget the moment when everything finally clicked.

The crippling weight of my years spent trying to gain favor and approval in His sight was suddenly gone and replaced with a new understanding. I had a humbling understanding that the Christian faith is not works-based, but instead a marvelous gift from the Lord. I experienced a life-changing understanding that God's acceptance would never be something I could ever muster up on my own because it was something that came as a result of His grace alone. This incredible truth deepened and strengthened in my heart when I embraced the gift of Bible literacy.

As I dove beneath the surface of Scripture, my old understanding of who I believed God to be was met with the new and right understanding of who He truly was. He had not hidden who He was. I sought this understanding in all the wrong places growing up. I finally found that it had been in the one thing I neglected and needed most all along: God's Word. As the understanding of my brokenness and desperate need for God's grace began to grow and humble me, the true, incomparable beauty of the Gospel wrecked me in all the right ways.

Rather than being driven by fear and pride, I found myself led by wonder and awe. I began to focus on living my life in such a way that yielded itself to the truth that I am freely accepted by God and nothing can change that. The victory had already been won, and it had nothing to do with what I could do, but rather what had been done for me and you.

God knew my fight for His favor was impossible. I was chasing the wrong path when the true way had already been paved by Christ Jesus, who took on flesh and bore our punishment for not keeping the law. Jesus fulfilled our requirement to keep the law, so that in Christ we have a punishment and a perfection that is complete.

God is for us, not because we follow the path of law-keeping, but only because we are a people in Christ. As Galatians 2:16 tells us, "*We know that a person is not justified by works of the law but through faith in Jesus Christ*" (ESV). May we rejoice and live our lives in such a way that reflects this humbling and glorious truth.

Reflection with Gina:

> "When you pass through the waters, I will be with you, and the rivers will not overwhelm you. When you walk through the fire, you will not be scorched, and the flame will not burn you."
>
> —Isaiah 43:2 (CSB)

As I write this devotional, I am sitting on the rocks at one of my favorite spots in Ohio, Marblehead Lighthouse. Anyone who knows me personally or has been around the ministry knows how much I love this place! This is a place where I find peace and where I connect with God in a real way. I love staring out at the place where the water seems to meet the sky and how the water crashes perfectly into the rocks. I am watching the geese and the ducks as the waves are coming in. They are sitting on the water, just allowing the waves to come in, fully trusting that they will not sink or drown, even if the waves get a little heavier or taller.

I'm reminded of how legalism can feel like a flood or fire, overwhelming us with rules and rituals that weigh us down. But just as God promises to be with us through the waters and fires, He also offers freedom from the chains of legalism. Legalism tells us that we must do more, be more, or follow a strict set of rules to earn God's favor. But this verse reminds us that it is God who carries us, not our own efforts.

When we trust fully in God, just like those geese trust the waves, we can let go of trying to earn His love or approval through our actions. Instead, we rest in the truth that His grace is sufficient, and His presence is enough to guide us through any challenge. God is our anchor in the storms (Hebrews 6:19) and our refiner in the fire (1 Peter 1:7).

Questions:

1. In what ways have you found yourself bound by legalistic thinking, and how does understanding God's promise to be with you in every trial help you break free from those constraints? How can you lean on His grace instead of striving to measure up?

2. How have you experienced God's presence during times when you felt overwhelmed by life's pressures? Can you see how He guided you through those waters or fires, even when it felt like you were on the verge of being overwhelmed?

3. Reflecting on the idea of trusting God in the face of challenges, what does it look like for you to trust Him fully, even when the waves of life seem too strong or the fire too intense?

Prayer:

God, I pray that as I walk out this Christian life, I would remember to keep my focus on You. Not on what other people say I should be doing or not doing. Not on following a set of guidelines, but focusing on the relationship. I want to put all of my trust and belief in who You are and the grace You have shown me through Jesus's death, burial and resurrection. In Jesus's name, Amen.

"When you pass through the waters, I will be with you, and the rivers will not overwhelm you. When you walk through the fire, you will not be scorched, and the flame will not burn you"

ISAIAH 43:2
(CSB)

Chapter 20

Falling Into Surrender

By Benny DiChiara

I am not fragile, yet I understand the fragility of life. I am not lost, but I know the aimless paths of those who wander. I am not a victim, but I have experienced life-saving salvation from the inside out. My world has been shaken, but my feet are planted firmly on the strongest of foundations. Even as I faced an abyss of the unknown, I never did so alone. God was always with me.

In October 2015, I endured a traumatic brain injury (TBI) that placed my life and future in peril. A fall sent me to the emergency room and ICU with a concussion and closed fracture of the skull base with subarachnoid, subdural, and extradural hemorrhages. The catastrophic injury could have easily ended my life or, at the least, compromised the quality of it. But God…I remember absolutely nothing from the first month after my injury; it's just gone. Once I started to come out of it, I experienced memory gaps, speech problems, and walking issues.

Everything looked surreal. The battle for my life and mind was not easy or quick. During the struggles, I clung to the knowledge that the battle for my heart had already been won. I compare the experience to someone who is just lost and feels as though they cannot find their way. You have no answers. But then, there was Jesus. Hand in hand with my Savior, I not only defied medical odds (miraculously), but I discovered and plumbed the depths of burgeoning creative inspiration that merged into the most recent music from my band, Empowered.

As I recovered, the injury did not affect my ability to make music. I was afraid I would lose that gift, but instead, He elevated that gift. God not only restored and magnified my musical gifts, but He also provided backup through the latest iteration of my band, Empowered. The members include Shane Madere Jr. (lead guitarist, backing vocalist), Jeff Maddox (a prodigy on bass, backing vocals), Mic Capdeville (killer percussionist, backing vocalist), and Justin Burdette (guitars, backing vocals). Their talent, alongside my newly acquired resolve and insight, coalesced and put to song the miracle of salvation, the joy of purpose, and the unshakable, unequivocal victory that Christ claimed when He rose on the third day. There is a lot going on in this world, and people are still searching for the Truth. Our project begins with this simple truth—no matter what is going on in your life, no matter what Satan is throwing at you, God takes care of it. Jesus was crucified, died, buried, and rose again for all of us. Amazingly, He did it all in just three days!

Once someone hears and is touched in any way by the message of God's love, it's their duty to empower others with that message. It is a duty that I assume with pride and intentionality as one who knows first-hand the emptiness of a life lived apart from Christ. While I was raised in church, the truth of redemption eluded my heart and mind for years. I considered myself a Christian but had no idea what being a Christian meant. I was born in New Orleans, Louisiana, the eldest of six children. We were raised in a liturgical church. I even served as an acolyte. All those years, I learned a lot about Jesus, but I did not *know* Jesus.

It would be a while before a genuine relationship with my Savior took shape. I spent four years in the U.S. Navy as a hospital corpsman, enjoyed success with a regional secular rock band, and started a family. Over time, however, pieces of my life began to unravel, including my marriage. Divorce after more than ten years was one of the hardest things I have ever gone through. Man, do I wish that I had truly known Jesus at that time—I believe things could have turned out differently. Five years following the divorce, I was working as a floor manager for a local automobile dealership when one of our clients invited me to church. Then she asked again and again. Eventually, I agreed to attend a service at what was then known as Trinity Christian Center in Baton Rouge, Louisiana. Thank God for that sweet lady's persistence (Ms. Linda). I loved the music. I loved the message. I felt God was speaking directly to me. At the end of the service, I went forward during the altar call and gave my life to Jesus, and my life has never been the same since! From that point, I've surrendered every aspect of my world to Jesus. All these years later, I'm still in awe of the mighty works God set into motion.

Because of His faithfulness, Empowered has become a staple of the live music scene in our home state of Louisiana and across the country, having shared the stage with such powerhouse artists as Switchfoot, MercyMe, 7eventh Time Down, and Jaci Velasquez. Our latest releases have generated more than 360,000 streams on Spotify alone, while the single *"Listen to the Children"* debuted at #5 on IndieGospel.net's popular show, "T. Roy Taylor's Top 20 Countdown."

The success is indicative of the music's relevance and poignancy for such a time as this. Society is bombarding our kids with messages that are the antithesis of the gospel. We need to counter with our faith and give our kids strong, Godly guidance on these issues. But we cannot do that without communicating. We need to listen to our children so we can hear what the world is telling them and counter it with the gospel of Jesus Christ. Jesus is our rock. The good news is that no matter how far down you fall, you do not have to live there. Sometimes, we get caught up in our own little worlds and fail to see what God has in store for us on a deeper, more personal level. It's like living inside of a snow globe—all you see is snow when your world gets shaken. It takes someone outside of the snow globe to show us the bigger picture, and that's what God does. For the last eight years, I've had quite a view, not to mention more than one shake-down. Even now, my TBI and its cause remain somewhat of a mystery while the effects are lingering.

The doctors never did figure out why my fall occurred. But, thank God, I mostly recovered. There are a few after-effects—I have an occasional memory lapse, and I have no sense of taste or smell due to the frontal lobe crush that happened during the fall. Ultimately, though, this event has only strengthened my relationship with Christ. There is something in the silence and peace that He brings in this type of situation. I always thought that God's voice was this huge, booming command. I found that it's gentle, caring, loving, compassionate, and understanding. It's peace. There is no doubt that He saved me for a reason. He spoke it into me with the knowledge that He was, is, and always will be there for me. God used this in my life to teach me not to be afraid. I know that He saved my life and that He has a plan for my life. I am not afraid to be bold in representing Him now.

Reflection with Gina:

> "Jesus told him, 'I am the way, the truth, and the life. No one comes to the Father except through me.'"
> —John 14:6 (CSB)

These words from Jesus are a powerful declaration of who He is and what He offers us. When we talk about healing—whether it's physical, emotional, or spiritual—it all begins with knowing Jesus as the way, the truth, and the life.

Healing isn't just about recovering from pain or sickness; it is about finding wholeness in Christ. Jesus didn't just come to fix our brokenness temporarily; He came to give us life and life abundantly. The abundant life is rooted in the understanding that He is the only way to true healing. Jesus offers us permanent, deep, and transforming healing from the inside out.

When we fully embrace Jesus as the way, the truth, and the life, we begin to see that our healing is not just about the absence of pain but about the presence of God's peace, joy, and purpose. He leads us on the path of healing by showing us the truth about who we are in Him and who He is for us.

If you're seeking healing today, I encourage you to lay everything at his feet. Let Him be your way when you feel lost, your truth when you're surrounded by lies, and your life when you feel drained and weary. He is the only one who can bring the true healing for which your soul longs.

Questions:

1. Reflect on a time when you experienced healing through your relationship with Jesus. How did acknowledging Him as the way, the truth, and the life impact that journey?

2. If you have not experienced the true power of Christ that Benny talks about, what is stopping you?

3. In what areas of your life are you seeking healing right now? How can you intentionally invite Jesus to be the way, the truth, and the life in those specific areas?

Prayer:

God, You know about all the areas of my life that are in need of healing. It is so difficult for me to relinquish control of every area of my life. I want to have all of the answers and the cures right now for each ailment in my body and my mind. I open my hands to You and give You full control. I want to have the faith to know that You will work all things according to Your good and perfect will. Help my unbelief. In Jesus's name, Amen.

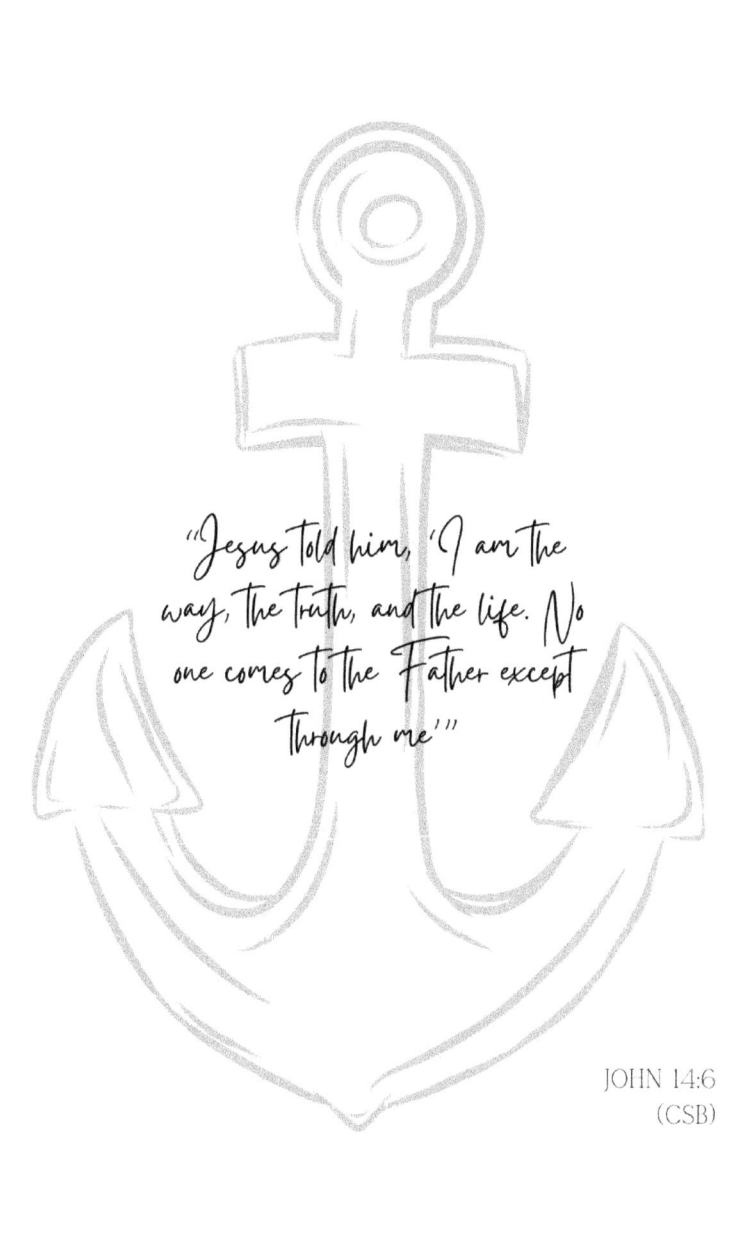

Chapter 21

Healing From Shame

by Inés Franklin

When I was putting together the final chapters of this book, I kept feeling this nudge in my heart to have someone share the story of their healing journey after having an abortion. Ines's name kept coming to my mind and spirit, so I reached out to her. She gave me permission to include an excerpt from Chapter 7, pages 134-136, in her book, *Uncharted*[1], so you will find someone who has been through what you have gone through and know you are not alone. God can forgive you, so hand it to Him and let Him begin the work of forgiving yourself.

As I write this chapter, my social media feed is flooded with posts about the recent ruling by the Supreme Court of the United States (SCOTUS). On June 24, 2022, SCOTUS overturned the 1973 landmark legal decision that held a woman's right to an abortion as a federal right protected by the Fourteenth Amendment to the Constitution and thus was a legally protected procedure across the United States. As of the time of this writing, abortion is no longer a federal constitutional right. Each

---

1. Franklin, Ines. (2023). *Uncharted: Navigating Your Unique Journey of Faith.* Fedd Books

state now has the responsibility to decide whether abortions are allowed within its borders and under what conditions. Emotions run high over this ruling and subject. News outlets and social interactions are peppered with arguments from both sides. Images and words take our breath away as people express their raw emotions and passionate perspectives.

In the meantime, in the silence of my writing room, I am thinking of my two babies, Micah and Angel.

I named them at an abortion recovery class. The pastor in charge of this beautiful program was unable to attend the last session of the class, and he asked me to fill in for him. He had heard my story and thought I would be an especially empathetic pastor to the participants who were about to do the most difficult part of the course. The goal of the last class is to help the parent(s) release their unborn, aborted children to the Lord and to rest in God's grace, mercy, and love through Jesus.

At first, I complained to the recovery pastor, reminding him that I had never been through a recovery class of this type. I had not yet processed the two abortions I underwent as a young adult. And although I did not share this with him, I lived with deep, unhealthy shame as well as sadness about my actions. However, he insisted I could pastor these people on this important day. Fueled by his encouragement, I went.

My role was to tell my story, name my children, and join others as we released a single balloon with a name tag for each child. Each class participant had family members with them for this important day. In small groups, they spread out around the church chapel and found a place to cry, embrace, and release their babies. I was alone and lost my pastoral composure as my two white balloons ascended into the sky and disappeared behind clouds. A woman saw me sobbing and came to my rescue, helping me find my composure to finish the session in prayer.

Micah (or Michaela) was conceived when I was eighteen years old, the first time I had sex with my boyfriend. Deep shame. I could not tell my mother, and I certainly was not about to tell my siblings. My boyfriend told me an abortion was the only option and that we were too young to be parents. My mother was oblivious to my plan when I asked her for the one hundred and fifty dollars I needed for the procedure.

Angel (or Angela) was conceived when I was twenty-three years old, less than a year after my first divorce when I was still dating my soon-to-be second husband. He was out of town when I found out, and I knew he would not be happy, so I took care of it before he found out. He was so sad when I told him. Deeper shame. It saddens me that both children were conceived with men I later married. My son and my daughters have siblings they never met. My older sister cried when she found out. Through a well of tears, she told me that she would have gladly raised my children. Other than her son, she was unable to get pregnant again, and her heart ached for more children.

Abortion was not my only option.

Shame compounds. Sadness is still in my heart. It is impossible to talk about this and not feel my heart break into a million little pieces yet again. So what did I do? What do I do? All that awful, humiliating shame that says, "You are bad," I give it to Jesus. By his costly grace, I am no longer condemned.

Were it not for Jesus, I would never tell you this story. My preference is to hide and cover up my pain. I did that for years. But I didn't just surrender my babies to Jesus. I actively surrendered my life. The Lord prompted me to share my story publicly many years ago. But first, I spent a lot of time in prayer, sought wise counsel, journaled, and talked to my family and friends. Not every person needs to tell the details of their story, as I have here. But I pray that by sharing how I reflected in my ugliest, you will be encouraged to surrender unhealthy shame and walk the faith journey in freedom. Jesus wants this freedom for you. But even if you struggle to do so today, know that he is pursuing you daily. Jesus is like the man in his parable who leaves the ninety-nine sheep in search of his one lost sheep, and he keeps looking until he finds it and brings it back on his shoulders, rejoicing.

Reflection with Gina:

> "We proclaim him, warning and teaching everyone with all wisdom, so that we may present everyone mature in Christ. I labor for this, striving with his strength that works powerfully in me."
>
> —Colossians 1:28–29 (CSB)

In Inés's story, she talks about how her pastor called her out to do something that made her feel uncomfortable, and she didn't feel ready for it. She could not see it at the time, but by her saying yes, she was able to finally break free from the shackles of shame that had held her for so long.

I am sure Paul felt the same way when he met Jesus on the road to Damascus. He had spent so long persecuting and killing followers of Jesus that he could not understand why Jesus would speak to him and call him out. He could not see the bigger picture.

In this section of Colossians, Paul is talking about his ministry and about the importance of proclaiming Jesus to others and not listening to the false teachings going on during that time. He talks in the surrounding verses about having the Gentile believers come to know God's mystery, which is Christ in each person and the hope of his glory (v. 27).

God has placed each of us in the place we are in now for such a time as this (Esther 4:14). He has entrusted us with the wisdom to help Christians not be "baby" Christians for their whole lives, but that first must start with us. We have to take an honest look at our own relationship with God to determine where we are. We cannot teach others from a place of spiritual immaturity. So, let's go to God today in humility and honesty about where we are in our walk with Him and where things need to change.

Questions:

1. Take an honest inventory of your spiritual walk. Not in how long you have been walking with Jesus, but in the condition of the relationship with Him.

2. Are you still drinking milk that someone else gives you? Are you starting to dig slightly and puree your diet of His Word? Are you in the meat and potatoes phase where you are digging into the Word and living it out on a daily basis? Are you somewhere in between? (1 Corinthians 3:2)

3. What is your next step toward spiritual maturity? Where is God calling you to minister and which people need to hear from you? Begin by looking at the stage of life you are in and where He has you placed.

Prayer:

God, today I come before You and admit that I am not where I need to be to do the work You have called me to do. I repent and I hand it over to You. I ask for You to lead me where You are calling me to be. Reveal to me exactly what my next steps are to fulfill Your plan to reach the people You have called me to reach. Remind me it is not in my power or strength that I walk, but it is in Yours. Help me to see what is going on where You have placed my feet. It is not all about me; it is about the souls of the people around me. In Jesus's name, Amen

"We proclaim him, warning and teaching everyone with all wisdom, so that we may present everyone mature in Christ. I labor for this, striving with his strength that works powerfully in me"

COLOSSIANS 1:28-29
(CSB)

Chapter 22

Healing Is Not Just Physical

by Gina Fox

You have reached the final chapter of this book! I wanted to talk about two of my healing journeys to close it out; one being with my dad and the last one being my own journey. You may ask why I am combining these two into one section, but I believe you will have your answer at the end.

Healing with My Dad

I know my life, just like yours, can be separated into stages. I talked a lot about my mom and our history back in Chapters 1 and 11 of this book, but I haven't talked much about the other person involved in that story. That person is my dad. Because of the situation my mom and I were in, there were many years, in fact, most of my 20s and early 30s, when I was without my dad. Let me go back to the beginning before we go there.

Growing up, I was a daddy's girl. I was the first child on both sides of the family, so I admit I was spoiled by everyone involved. My dad and I were especially close. The first thing I ever read was the sports page many years before "See Spot Run." We went to soccer, basketball, baseball and football games together. I was the athletic one between me and my brother. I gained my love of music from him as well. We would go to the local Eagles hangout when our favorite band, The Johnson Five, would play, and we would dance to multiple songs throughout the night. I was also a ballet dancer when the song "Ballerina Girl"[1] by Lionel Ritchie came out, and that was one of our favorites to dance to. There were so many amazing moments with him growing up and as a teenager. Yet, our relationship started to change during my late teens and early twenties. Sure, my teenage hormones and bad attitude had something to do with that, but it was mainly due to the relationship I had with my Mom and the advancement of her mental health issues. As I may have previously stated, when Mom needed a scapegoat, that was me. I would be the one who was blackballed from the family and ousted because I wouldn't bow down to her and didn't rely on her to help me. I eventually had to walk away from the toxicity, and that meant walking away from my dad.

He was supporting his wife, which is what men are told to do, but in doing that, I did not get to share many of my pivotal moments with him. I didn't get to have him at the graduation from my nursing program. I didn't get to have him walk me down the aisle at my wedding, and he wasn't there during the most difficult time of my infertility journey. I was heartbroken not to have him there and I know he was too.

But then, in 2013, Mom passed away. I received a call at work from my grandmother to let me know and that Dad wanted to see me. I left work and headed to the hospital, where the ambulance had taken my mom. I spent the rest of the day with him, writing her obituary and walking him

---

1. Richie, L. (1986). Ballerina Girl. On Dancing on the Ceiling [Song]. Motown

through the steps that we knew would happen but didn't think it would come at the age of 53.

We spent the next nine months working on our relationship. I finally got to take him to a Cleveland Indians game, just as I had always wanted to do since becoming a nurse. It was so much fun and I was so ecstatic to be there with him. Then in October 2013, I almost lost him too. He had a massive staph infection in his lower back and spine that was overlooked by the hospital. He was in the ICU, had major surgery and was confused for many months. All of a sudden, I was his medical power of attorney and making all kinds of decisions on his behalf. I was not in a good place with God at the time and told Him that He couldn't have my dad because I just got him back in my life and I wasn't ready to let him go yet. God worked through that situation to bring us a lot closer and changed how we perceived the precious lives we have been given.

Dad and I have been walking out our healing journey for the last 13 years. It has been difficult at times, but also so amazing! We had to have tough discussions and had to apologize to each other for what we had done. We have gone back to church, concerts, and sporting events, and we have even gotten to serve together at different events. It is the relationship I have always wanted with him! We have grown so close as adults that not only do I have my dad, but I also have an amazing friend!

My Personal Healing Journey

Now we come to the part of this section and book in which I talk about my own healing journey that led to the "Anchored by the Sword" ministry, podcast and now this book. I have written about my journey with mental health in Chapter 1 and how I could have so easily lost that battle. ***But***

God. I also talked about the grief and loss journey my husband and I went through with infertility in Chapter 7. ***But God***. Then, in chapter 11, I talked about surviving the loss of my mom and grandmother. ***But God***. The reason I say that is if it wasn't for Him, I would have never survived each of those events. God has been with me every step of the way, even when I couldn't see it.

At the end of 2019, I went to a local women's conference with one of my friends. I had heard about the speaker and her ministry before, but I wasn't ready at the time. She was speaking about becoming free from your past. She talked about an upcoming class called Unbound, which should start in 2020. I felt as though God was telling me it was time to deal with all the crap from my past so I could move forward in what He wanted me to do, so that is what I did.

I walked through a 13-week class where I finally dealt with the issues in my past. I walked through and broke the soul ties with abusive relationships, assault, sexual sin, pornography, hurt that I caused others, unforgiveness, bitterness and every other thing that was keeping me bound. I was finally free and healed while still in the process of healing. Stefanie taught me that important lesson. During the class, I had put Hebrews 6:19 on a block she had given us to put a verse to stand on during our journey. A couple of days after the soul-tie-breaking part of the class, I felt the phrase "Anchored by the Sword" impressed on my spirit. I didn't know what it meant, so I asked God. He let me know to start a Facebook page, create an icon and to start gathering information to start a website. So I did. Within five minutes, 20 people liked it. It grew from there.

After almost a year of trying to figure everything out, my friend Nikki told me I should start a podcast. I said, "No, I don't have time for that and no one would want to listen to me anyway." She told me to hold onto the idea. Less than two months later, I felt the urge to do it after a message popped up on my phone about a discussion being held by my friend, Merritt Onsa, asking, "Are you ready to start your podcast?" I joined the discussion and asked many questions. Then, a week later, I saw an online giveaway for podcast equipment. I entered and won the equipment. So I asked God, "Are you trying to tell me something?" I felt the confirmation and the idea for the podcast came to me while I was watching Wonder Woman[2]. That main fight scene will inspire anyone to take over the world and become free! So, in March of 2021, the "Anchored by the Sword" podcast started and is still going strong almost four years later.

Being able to share the freedom stories of my friends, colleagues, authors, entertainers, producers, directors and so many others has been the best journey I could have ever wanted. With every story I get to share, another part of me becomes healed. I feel another link break off the chains. God never promised us an easy path, but He promised to never leave us. My life is proof of this. Although complete and total healing won't happen until I see Jesus face to face, I can live in the assurance of His love, compassion, grace and faithfulness to lead me down the road He has set up for me until that day.

---

2. Jenkins, P. (Director). (2017). Wonder Woman [Film]. Warner Bros

Reflection with Gina:

> "This hope is a strong and trustworthy anchor for our souls. It leads us through the curtain into God's inner sanctuary."
> —Hebrews 6:19 (NLT)

As I stated, this verse was one of the "block" verses I stood on during my freedom journey that started in January 2020. I am a water person. Everyone who knows me in real life knows just how true this is. If you have seen some of my pictures online, then you know just how much I am infatuated with water and lighthouses. I have spent some amazing years in Marblehead, Ohio, with my family. I have the most peace in my life when I am up at Lake Erie. I was introduced to Lakes Michigan and Huron in October of 2023, so my peace is expanding!

This is why I can relate so well to this passage in a visual way. I can see the anchor keeping the boats in place and strong against the waves and the storms that pound into it at every angle. I have been beaten down by people and situations and have felt like I could not breathe or take another step. I have felt the drowning pressure of waves and wondered if I would survive, both physically and figuratively. On June 1, 1996, I took my first steps by inviting Jesus to save me and guide me out of the storms and begin to tell me who I really am. Ever since then, it has been a journey of me drowning, flailing out to Jesus to save me again, and finally learning how to trust that the Anchor will keep me in place. Even when I am battered, bruised and barely breathing, He is there and He will never let go. I have grown to have trust in the strong, steadfast arms of our God. I will continue to learn this through whatever the storms of life will throw at me.

Questions:

1. What does it mean to you personally that hope is described as a "strong and trustworthy anchor" for your soul? Reflect on moments in your life when you've felt anchored in this hope, especially during challenging times.

2. How do you experience God's presence when you lean into the hope that leads you "through the curtain into God's inner sanctuary"? Consider how this hope shapes your relationship with God and how it draws you closer to Him in your daily walk.

3. In what areas of your life do you need to be reminded that God's hope is your anchor? Think about situations where you might be struggling to hold on to hope and how this verse can encourage you to trust in God's promises.

Prayer:

God, I confess that I have let the storms of life beat me down. I have let the opinions of others and their actions dictate my reactions more than trusting in You. I repent of this and ask You to reach out Your hand to me so I can grab ahold of it with everything I have. Thus, I allow You to carry the heaviness of what has been weighing me down. Remind me to place my trust in You. Help me know You will keep me anchored through the storms I will face and the life You are creating for me. You never promised an easy life, but You did promise that You would always be with me. Thank you for being my Protector, my Anchor and the One on whom I can always depend. In Jesus's name, Amen.

"This hope is a strong and trustworthy anchor for our souls. It leads us through the curtain into God's inner sanctuary."

HEBREWS 6:19
(NLT)

Conclusion

"And they have defeated him by the blood of the Lamb and by their testimony."

—Revelation 12:11a (NLT)

God knew the end of the story. He knew where you and I would be at this very moment. Although He never wanted any of the bad things to happen, He never left us. In fact, He created each of us for a specific reason at this time in history for a purpose. He knew the people we would be sent to reach at this time. We have gone or are going through our own personal hell so we can help people who are or have gone through the same things find their way to God. It's weird to think of it in those terms, but think about the people in your life. Think about the people who have had the greatest impact on you. God has created each person with their own set of gifts to impact the kingdom. Looking back at each of the stories, do you think any of us wanted to battle these things? I will say first, "***NO!***"

But God. God met each of us and brought us to a point where we realized just how much we really needed Him. Whether that was at the age of 5 or in our 30s, each story matters. He has a plan for each of us.

It was not a coincidence that you picked up this book! Whether you know God or don't care to know Him, He loves you more than you will ever know. He has never set out to hurt you; we live in a world where bad things happen. He wants to hold you close under His wings and protect you. God doesn't want people to die or not know Him. He has so many good gifts to give to each of you and it starts with giving Jesus your heart and truly repenting for what has happened. Then dive into His Word and ask Him to show you what is next. He is able to do all things and guide you through each part of your life. Live with open hands, an open mind and an open heart. God will lead you to a place where you never thought you would be. Life is not about money or material things; it is about the internal work He does to produce the external results not just for your benefit, but for the people He will impact through you.

"And they have defeated him by the blood of the Lamb and by their testimony."

REVELATION 12:11A
(NLT)

Acknowledgments

First of all, I have to give all glory and honor to **God.** I could have never survived everything I went through without Your hand on me. Thank you for saving me, giving me the opportunity to do what You have called me to do, and for not letting me keep saying no! This is all about You because of You, and I give it to You! Thank you for not letting the worst parts of my story go to waste.

Matthew Fox — My husband and my soulmate, thank you for encouraging me throughout this entire process and for being the one to make me realize that even though it has been difficult, this was the book I was supposed to write. You were the first one many years ago to tell me that someone may want to read what I had to say when I first started talking about writing a book long before the ministry, podcast, and the idea for this book was ever born. Thank you for being with me over the last 25 years and for loving me, even through my crazy! I am so grateful for the gift you have been and continue to be. I Love you and give you *All My Love.*

Jim Payne — I am so thankful that you are my dad! You have supported me since I first picked up a sports page at 18 months old and couldn't understand a word I was reading, but you helped me discover my love of reading and sports. Thank you for allowing me to share parts of our story and for encouraging me to keep on going when I would doubt myself or when I wondered if this is truly what I was called to do. I love you!

Roger and Rose Varn — Thank you for all of your support over the 25 years since I came storming into your lives. You guys supported me at times when no one else did. Thank you for raising a great son that I get to call my husband. I pray blessings over you both!

To My Nephews: Ryan, Dylan, Cody, Kyle and Aiden — You are five of the reasons why I want to love and serve God with everything I am. I know you may not understand it now, or I haven't always done the best job, but I want to leave a legacy of trusting in God and believing that He is who He says He is and He will do what He says He will do. He gave me each one of you to demonstrate how I could be a large part of raising children without actually giving birth to them. You are each sons of the Most High God and He has so many good things in store for you. Just trust and believe in Him. He's got you! Also, thank you to my brother and sister-in-law, ***Craig and April Payne,*** for allowing me to be a large part of their lives and for giving me the best gifts I could have asked for.

Lacy Grace — You are an amazing gift from God in my life. I have told you many times how I have considered you more family than a friend. God knew I would need someone who was not afraid to battle for me and with me in both the physical and spiritual realms. I could not have gotten through the writing of this book and also the last six years without you! Thank you for not only being my "soul sister" but for inviting me into your family, I am so grateful for your friendship, and I love you, sis!

Khloe — You are one of the gifts that has come out of my friendship with your mom. You are beautiful daughter of the King, and He has such an amazing call on your life! You make me smile and laugh with your fun videos, and make me cry when you tell me about the impact I have had on you. Well, girl, it goes both ways! I love you, niece!

To the OG "Aunt Pack," — ***Danielle Amigo, Ashley Dotson, Lacy Velton and Melinda Lee-*** Thank you for accepting me, flaws and all, from the beginning when I forced myself into your group at Faith Family! I love each of you and have loved doing life with you all! I prayed for a group of friends who would accept me fully, even when I brought Honey

Roasted BBQ sauce from CFA to a Hibachi restaurant! I knew y'all were keepers then! I pray for God to rain down His blessings on each of you.

Also, I am so grateful for our newest Aunt Pack members, **Alexis Kimble, Sussie Pineda and Carrie Nyholm!** You girls are amazing, and I am loving that you are a part of my life now. Also let's keep picking out concerts to serve at together!

Christa Crookston — What can I say about you?! You are the epitome of what a true friend and supporter is. From the moment I told you and Dave about Anchored by the Sword to when I asked you to contribute to the book and be a part of the ABTS team, you have always been there to support me, even during the darkest moments of your life. You are a true light and one of the strongest people I know. You are doing an amazing job and having a major impact on Addie and Aidyn, as well as the bigs. I know the blessings of Heaven will rain down on you and also be waiting for you in Heaven! I love you so much!

Nikki Osborne — None of this happens without you! It started all the way back in 1996 when you befriended me and showed me the love of God. Your invitation to church led me to where I am today. Also, the podcast and the book would not be here if it wasn't for you challenging me to the idea of starting a podcast months before it came to be. Thank you for still sticking with me through the ups and downs of the last 28+ years. I am so grateful for our friendship and also for you being a part of the ABTS team!

Thank you to everyone who has helped to make this project possible through your prayers and contributions!

Thank you to all of the amazing **contributors** to this book and guests on the "Anchored by the Sword" podcast! Thank you for allowing me to be the conduit in which you chose to share your story. You all are so brave, and I appreciate you more than you know!

Special Thanks to...

Andrea Lende and **Jodi Howe** for encouraging me throughout this process of self-publishing. Your continued encouragement throughout this self publishing journey has been invaluable! I am so grateful for your confidence in me!

Thank you to **Sarah Geringer** and **Ruth Hovsepian** for walking me through the editing and formatting of this book! I could not have done any of this without your expertise and patience with me! I pray so many blessings on you both!

Thank you to my incredible launch team for helping me get this book in front of so many people I could not have reached otherwise!

Contributor Information

Jodi Howe: Jodi Howe lights up any stage or digital platform with her dynamic energy and heartfelt messages as an accomplished author, award-winning podcaster, and sought-after speaker. Passionate about writing and music, she inspires others through her video blogs, prayers, and role as a vocal coach and church worship team member. Based in Cary, North Carolina, Jodi embraces a life of creativity, purpose, and connection while cherishing her role as a devoted mother.

Scott Box: Scott Box is the founder of the ministry, Worship Hero. His mission is to change the way people understand and practice worship by providing tools to "Pursue Jesus. Reflect Jesus." as a habit leading to hope; to live lifestyles of heroic disgrace. He lives in Central Oregon with his wife Kariann, daughter Ainsley and son Titus. They share their home with a four-pound dog that has no teeth.

Kim Gentry Meyer: Mrs. Massachusetts 2020, award-winning songwriter and poet Kim Gentry Meyer is also an International Acoustic Music Award winner and a finalist in the USA Songwriting Competition. She is also an accomplished visual artist and painted the album cover art for her debut project, "Herald," which was recently released from NWN Records and Integrated Music Rights, part of the Integrity Music family. She and her husband, Adam, currently live on Cape Cod with a home full of personally rescued dogs and cats.

Cally Logan: Cally Logan is an author and Senior Writer for Crosswalk. She has been featured on shows such as The 700 Club Interactive, and her writing has appeared in numerous outlets, including Christine Caine's Propel Women. Cally served as a mentor for young women for several years and enjoys challenging ladies to develop deeper relationships with God and to live fearlessly and authentically. She received her B.A. Degree from Regent University. In her spare time, she enjoys spending time in nature, genuine connection chats over coffee, and woodworking.

Wendy Blight: Wendy Blight's heart's desire is to help women fall in love with God's Word. To learn it, pray it, and know with confidence they can tackle any problem life presents through it. Wendy serves as the Biblical Content Specialist for Proverbs 31 Ministries and has authored five books. Wendy and her family live in Charlotte, North Carolina, and her favorite times are when they all gather together on her back porch.

Grace Wabuke Klein: Grace Wabuke Klein and her husband lead focus412, a ministry that helps leaders and churches grow. For over fifteen years, Grace was on the pastoral leadership team at Faith Church. She has been a guest on numerous media outlets, including the 700 Club, LIFE Today, Proverbs 31 Ministries, Live Original with Sadie Robertson, The Writing Room with Bob Goff, and Propel Women. Grace received her bachelor's from UC Berkeley and her master's from Fuller Theological Seminary. Her greatest joy is spending time with her husband and their one-year-old grandson.

Lacy Grace: Lacy Grace is a wife and mother. She was a nurse for 17 years and recently stepped out of nursing to follow what God called her to do. She started working for a non-profit organization that helps women transition from prison back into society and helps women to know that they are loved by God and others. She also works part-time for another close friend at her business.

Amy Joob: Amy Joob is an award-winning author, speaker, and podcaster. She is a former model turned advocate. Her latest book is a 40-Day prayer journal titled, *Unstuck: Step into the New*. Her son Ashton was diagnosed with a rare genetic disorder in 2017 at the age of seven and it changed the trajectory of her family. She started her podcast, "Support Someone Saturday," in 2020, which highlights charities, ministries, and nonprofits. She encourages individuals and families to advocate and serve one another and those in need in Chicago and around the U.S. She leads a Moms in Prayer group at Willow Creek in Huntley and is involved with her husband, Eric, in Chicagoland United in Prayer. She and her husband help lead prayer in the northwest suburbs of Chicago and facilitate their online prayer meetings as well.

Brit Eaton: Brit Eaton is a writer, teacher, spiritual director, and all-around pursuer of the Kingdom of God. She helps corporate, nonprofit, and ministry leaders find the words to say to move people to action through coaching and consulting. An eager apostle and strong advocate for nontraditional recovery and women in ministry, Brit ministers in diverse, spirit-filled environments committed to unity in the Body of Christ.

Christa Crookston: Through a divorce, brain injury, career change, loss of her spouse, and cancer, God has been by her side, ever-present and ever-faithful. She holds a Business Administration Degree from the University of Akron and loves being able to utilize her skills while being a stay-at-home mom.

Kat Vazquez: Kat Vazquez is an award-winning journalist, author, TV host, producer and speaker. Her passion highlights how God weaves his storyline into humanity's. Kat has authored *REIGN: Restoring Identity* and co-authored *Your Story Is Not Done.* She and her husband, Jorge, have produced two TV series: "The Revolution TV" and "Your Story Is Not Done." They are a husband and wife ministry team called to evangelize the lost, energize and equip the body, while empowering believers to do the same. Kat and Jorge have two boys and currently live in Florida.

George A. Wood: George A. Wood is an ordained minister, pastoral care counselor, recovery ministry founder, and recovery activist. A former addict and suicide survivor, George has dedicated his life to radically grace-laced, Christ-centered recovery for people struggling with addictions, mental health problems, and suicidal thoughts. Through coaching and speaking, he helps people see recovery differently and build a new baseline for trauma-informed care.

Lindsay Griswold: Lindsay Griswold is a wife and mom to three children. She has a small business called *Find Wondrous Things*, which aims to create beautiful tools that encourage you to find the wonder of Christ and declare truth over your day.

Heather Creekmore: Heather Creekmore writes and speaks hope to thousands of women each week through her books, coaching, and podcast titled "Compared to Who?" Heather's heart is to encourage women who struggle with body image and comparison issues and help them find the freedom to stop comparing and start living.

Micah Lynn Hanson: Micah Lynn Hanson was born in Costa Mesa, California, but moved to the small mountain town, Coeur d' Alene, Idaho, at a very young age. She looks forward to continuing to tell powerful and meaningful stories, through her acting as well as producing her own projects in the future.

Elle Cardel: Elle Cardel is a sinner saved by God's great redeeming love and grace, wife to her college sweetheart, Michael, and mother to their beautiful daughter Selah and son Aidan. She was born and raised in the South and lives in Tennessee with her wonderful family. Elle is a full-time coffee-sipper, word-writer, friend-hugger, book-reader, shower-singer, and

DIY-dreamer. Most importantly, she delights in encouraging women of faith to be proactive in their pursuit of knowing God and delighting in the truths of His Word. She does this by providing Gospel-centered resources through her global online women's ministry, Daughter of Delight.

Benny DiChiara: Singer/songwriter/survivor Benny DiChiara has a powerful testimony of God's mercy and healing that he loves to share. He has been sharing it all over the world, most recently on national and international media outlets, including The 700 Club, Cornerstone Television Network's flagship show, Hope Today, The NRB Network's award-winning TV show Babbie's House, and many more.

Inés Franklin: Inés Franklin completed a Master of Divinity at Fuller Theological Seminary and is the founder of Trochia Ministries, whose mission is to provide Christian discipleship. She serves as a teaching pastor at Mariners Church in Southern California. She and her husband, James Franklin, live in Irvine, California.

About Gina Fox and Anchored by the Sword

Gina Fox is a wife, fur mama, aunt to many, ministry leader, writer, speaker and podcaster. She is the founder of Anchored by the Sword Ministry and Podcast, which came out of her own journey toward freedom. She loves connecting with people through storytelling and helping them to discover freedom in their own lives. She lives in Ohio with her husband, Matthew and her four fur babies, Bandit, Rascal, Hazel and Royce.

Anchored by the Sword was created to encourage men and women to become anchored in God and experience real freedom found in His Word, our true sword. We believe that God's Word will never return void and that we can trust it as our anchor with anything we face. Scan the QR code below to learn more, subscribe to our emails, and listen to all of our podcast episodes.

www.ingramcontent.com/pod-product-compliance
Lightning Source LLC
Chambersburg PA
CBHW060946050426
42337CB00052B/1609